1-SEO Wanted

Improve Your Website Visibility.
Learn How to Submit Your Website to Search Engines and Web Directories.

Mary E. Monteiro

MentionMe Publishing
Boston, Massachusetts

Attention corporations, Educational Institutions and writing conferences: Take 20% off and use my book as fundraisers, premiums, or gifts. Please contact the publisher:

Mention Me Publishing
116 A Ward Street
Boston, Massachusetts 02120
www.1seowanted.com

Library of Congress Cataloging-in-Publication Data

ISBN 13: 978-0-9833485-0-4

Published by Mention Me, Boston, MA

Cover and Layout by Createspace

Contents

PREFACE

I decided to write this book in order to draw wide attention to the importance of Search Engines ("SE") and web directories upon the purchase of a website. This book provides information about web directory self-submissions and step-by-step detailed instructions on how to submit your website to major search engines and web directories such as, Google, Yahoo! and the Open Directory Project (ODP), for creating an Internet presence for your website. As you continue to read this book I hope you will come away with an understanding of how SE and web directories work and how important they are to website visibility success.

I seek to reach many diverse audiences. First and foremost, I am speaking to those who aspire to build their own website Internet presence, particularly to the owner of small companies capable of embracing the link-building campaign and creating value and customer relationships on a much wider plane. I also want to reach those creative entrepreneurs who have already ventured out onto the Internet and who, are looking for ways of experimenting with elements of a link-building campaign. More broadly, I want to address the general public, especially those who have detected a glimmer of some very new possibilities in Internet website building opportunities, and/or seeking stay-at-home on line jobs during a time of economic recession, but who are not yet sure what it may mean for their business or personal lives.

I want to be clear about my intentions. I want to provide all readers with an understanding of search engines and web directories as a way to help navigate the many challenges one can face after establishing a website, and how to self-promote that site with an aim toward optimal Internet presence.

PREFACE

Since I am no expert on search engine optimization, I have not embarked on an extended description and analysis of search engines and web directories initiatives. Instead, my focus is to provide detailed instructions for submitting a website to various search engines and web directories "on your own and in many cases, free of charge." Following these steps will help prospective customers find your website when searching for the product and/or service you are offering. While every effort has been given to make this book as complete and accurate as possible, considering the changing nature of the Internet, some of the information provided in this book may require updating at time of delivery. In particularly, chapter 8, "The List!"

DEDICATION

Thank you to everyone who made this book possible—my family, particularly my sister Maureen, who felt the book was so informative she would buy a dozen copies to give to her friends, to my wonderful mother, Elizabeth, who encouraged me to "become a doer and not a talker of doers", and to my son, Ross, for turning out the way I hoped he would—passionate, funny, and smart.

Thank you to Rodney Patmon, for his help with the first draft, and giving me the motivation to complete the final draft. Thank you to my friend Joya Z Baynes, for her patience, skills, and humor. Finally, to New York who has inspired me from our very first meeting, may our paths cross again some day soon?

Most of all, this book is dedicated to you, the reader, who is thinking of starting a new website venture or already setting out on the web site ownership adventure. Go for it! We are living in an exciting time for website ownership. I hope you'll seize the opportunity to increase your website's visibility, traffic and sales, for yourself, your own way. And I hope you'll enjoy it as much as I have.

Loving-kindness,

Mary E Monteiro

INTRODUCTION

To guide readers through this unfamiliar landscape, this book is divided into nine chapters. The first chapter, "The Invitation" describes how I got into the website business. It begins with an overview of my daylong Internet Marketing workshop of possibilities, pressure, ignorance and monetary loss.

Chapter two, "The Internet", gives a brief description of the history of the Internet and its potential. With this context in place, Chapter three, "Search Engines ("SE"),"gives an understanding of how the SE work and why every Internet business owner should want to register with them. Additionally, Search Engine marketing terms such as, keywords, keyword phrases, title tag and creative content are introduced. I also list seven prevalent search engines and web directories on the Internet today that offer a faster way of getting your websites found and index for a small investment.

Chapter four and five, "a brief history of Search Engine Optimization ("SEO")," and "hire, a Search Engine Optimizer (SEOs)" discuss the fundamental ways in which the emergence and spread of start-ups and underperforming websites on the Internet have altered traditional promoting strategies. New services such as optimize content, internal links, meta tags, backlinks, social media, press release etc, have also emerged.

I argue that SEO, especially those that a website owner can execute themselves, such as registering their website for free with search engine and submitting to web directories, or just plain common sense requests for reciprocal links from other webmasters and/or website owners, will be significantly beneficial and fun to do.

Moreover, I anticipate that many website owners may want to hire SEOs to promote their sites for them, so I included some Pros and Cons of SEOs services, vital information here!

Marketing a website on the Internet is not an option that webmasters or website owners can choose to ignore. SEO represent a profound change that will unalterably transform the Internet promotional land-scape and benefit only those who tackle it head on.

In chapter six, "PageRank?" I discuss the distinctive characteristics of PageRank, the important of targeted inbound links, the principles of a successful link strategy, which emphasizes the need to generate, con-nect, and lock in traffic over time.

In chapter seven, "The Open Directory Project", you'll find step-by-step instructions on how to submit a website to live web directories. Using the Open Directory Project (ODP) as a submission model, I'll walk you through the process on ODP's official website submission form, using Colonlove.com and TennisAve.com submission requests. I encourage you to continue the process of submission to over 800 prominent search engines and web directories that I compiled in Chapter eight.

Chapter eight titled, "The List", includes my compilation of over 800 search engines and web directories. Many of the search engines and web directories have free registration and are listed in descending order beginning with the free listing first, Google PageRank second and finally with the for fees listing. This is roll up your sleeve time…

Chapter nine, "Conclusion" brings my website ownership pursue and experience into perspective drawing out a silver lining with blue ink in retrospect. After a long pursue of website ownership, website mar-keting conferences, monetary spending, long customer support telephone conversations on how to build my website and SEOs trying to squeeze more money out of me to market the sites, spark a charge to embark on wanting SEO for myself and by myself. In the end, this book "1-SEO wanted" is exactly what I and every website business owner need.

Chapter 1
THE INVITATION

My interest in search engines and web directories has evolved over the last six years. It began in 2005, after accepting an invitation to an Internet Marketing Workshop. The only reason I attended was to obtain the free Business Organizer that the Company advertised along with the invitation. Hey, it was a $39.99 value! I convinced my friend to come with me. We also agreed in advance that we would not purchase any of the products that were being offered for sale. We'd listen to the sales pitch, get our free gifts and then head for the door. Well, the sales pitch was captivating and I must admit the thought of owning my own website on the Internet sounded pretty cool. As entrepreneurs we were excited to discover how we could use the Internet to broaden our marketing efforts, create income and sell products and/or services both nationally and internationally.

Three hours into the Internet Marketing workshop, my friend Joya and I had purchased a special package which included six complete website store building software licenses. A website is a collection of related web pages, including multimedia content, typically identified with common domain name, and published on at least one web server.

Websites have many functions and can be used in various fashions; a website can be a personal website, a commercial website for a company, a government website or a non-profit organization website. I had my "Mary-of-all-trades, master-of-them-all-what-the-hell" attitude, and Joya had her "solid-hair-salon product-line, let's-do-this" attitude, which in hindsight would explain her "quick-draw-of-the-pen-to-sign-on-the-dotted-line-of-the- contract" *aptitude!!* The personal consultant, who was positioned for us to speak to at the workshop, was very persuasive and persistent. Joya and I were not in consultation to discuss whether or not to buy, but rather to acknowledge that if the Internet was a superhighway, we knew that we definitely wanted to ride it; all night long. We had to know how many websites we really needed, and how many we could really afford.

Joya said, "six...remember it takes money to make money!" I only wanted three. "Let's start out slow and then press the pedal to the metal upon launching a site, when the opening comes." After all we were new entrepreneurs. Oh no! Correction. Actually, we were poor newbie entrepreneurs with what we thought were two solid ideas for Internet productions.

Mr. Cute Pants

I wanted to purchase the minimum number of websites only they were sold in sets of three or six. They wouldn't sell just one website. The workshop host, who I'll call "Mr. Cute Pants" would not sell us just one. Purchasing six meant buying into a concept he called "mirror sites" Mr. Cute Pants was in Joya's ear..."If you want to make more money, you will need at least four websites to mirror." So we decided to purchase six. Joya pleaded with me to look at this purchase with an "all-or-nothing" attitude. "Let's go for it, all or nothing!" The only thing that came to my mind when I heard "mirror sites" was "my mirror teaching my reflection at home on the wall in my bathroom how to recite, "I love you", five times a day."

The workshop host was all over Joya. He was really cute and so were his pants. You ever wonder why some of the cutest people run most of those workshops? "You love money don't you?" He asked Joya. But all she heard was, "Money Loves me" Bring in the mirrors, reflections of bait, as he hooked and sold to the over zealous pretty young ladies in the hotel banquet room corner.

THE INVITATION

Well, when Mr. Cute Pants announced that we had purchased SIX websites, all of the other attendees started purchasing as well..."Who's next?" And "How many?"

Mirror Sites

Unfortunately, we found out a year or so later that "mirror sites" are sufficient evidence for banning websites which employ this strategy on the Internet.

It turns out that search engines and web directories definition of mirror on the Internet is any website containing the same files (a mirror) but having different" URL" (universal reference link) to monopolize the traffic amongst two or more sites. The mirror theory is supposed to improve performance PageRank (chapter 6) and reliability (frequency) for your websites. Mirroring sites translate into more traffic and more money 24 hours a day/ 7 days a week, or as Mr. Cute Pants stated, "While you sleep!"

At the time of our website purchases our idea was this: I would build a Tennis Pro Shop and Joya would build a hair salon product shop on the Internet. Afterwards, we would mirror these sites to each other and within each site for an increase in traffic, Internet presence, and a very healthy bank account.

Ideally, every website owner wants visitors, traffic ''hits", high visibility and guaranteed sales. Six websites making us money right away, right?

Wrong! Before you shell out thousands of dollars, let me give you a note of caution: Mirroring of certain websites (I have seen Government sites permitted to mirror) is grounds for becoming banished from the search engines, permanently.

1-SEO WANTED

Our plan for these purely for-profit websites fell into this banned category; something Mr. Cute Pants forgot to mention to us at the Internet Marketing workshop. Talk about take the money and run! So, we had two websites to build and four websites to sell! Joya felt miserable about the unnecessary purchase of six websites and, worst of all, she did not even get a kiss from that fine Mr. Cute Pants, whom we envision sipping tropical drinks at an all exclusive hotel paid for by people like us!

The mirror site strategy offered at the workshop was a quick money making scam to sell six websites for the presenting company and a potentially quick money making strategy for the website owners to increase traffic and sales. But that strategy came with serious consequences. Please understand, it is not illegal to mirror websites but it is consistently frown upon by the search engines operators. Additionally, it undermines your website's Internet presence; because the search engines will remove you from their index without even notifying you.

Seriously speaking! Is there anyone interested in the purchase of one fully loaded website storefront?

Please contact, **www.1seowanted.com**. It's not easy coming up with six winners; we only had two winning websites. Let's talk.

New Goals

Since Joya and I now had six website storefronts licenses, we turned our ideas into goals:

1. Build two successful websites,
2. Sell four websites, and
3. Get a return on investment "ROI"

I built TennisAve.com and Joya set out to build SalonList.com. With no money under our pillows and waking up to zero visitors from one live website, our new Internet venture was not showing any promise.

In addition to this, the self-serving hosting company, (whom name shall remain nameless, but whom story sounds familiar) which sold us the websites, wanted an additional $3,000 to build and manage the data base necessary to complete SalonList.com.

This purchase was not going to happen! So we stayed live with TennisAve.com (TA took me over a year to build) and we sat on the other five websites. Although I believe there were potential customers looking for my tennis products on the Internet (because I have many of the same products as other tennis websites) and were perhaps ready to buy my tennis products but ultimately could not locate TennisAve.com on the Internet.

How do people find a website on the Internet?

Location has become very important on the Internet as well. Strategically speaking, profitability of any business venture is displayed in its bottom line.

However, even with the perfect website, you will still need to promote your website beyond mere publication. Many website owners believe just getting the website up and running is the end of the process. I was one of them. The fact of the matter is that the real work begins when the website goes live! Simply throwing up a website, crossing your fingers and sitting around waiting for the traffic to pick up and orders to come in will guarantee your website's failure. I began to wonder, why an estimated 1.5 billion worldwide Internet users would not be able to randomly find my website. With a brick and mortar storefront business, you have a physical location (with an address) where customers can come to shop. On the Internet, I wanted to know, "How do people find my business?"

I discovered the answer for myself, one brick at a time! For website owners who are selling a product or a service, the answer to this question is obviously imperative. How do potential customers make a choice to buy products online if they cannot locate the website? Or equally bad-don't know it exists.

TennisAve.com had been live in cyberspace for over a year but with very little sales. I have to confess that I did have a bit of a "stand-apart" mentality as I approached the Internet revolution. As I sat in the hotel listening to Mr. Cute Pants ramble about making money as you sleep, I began to daydream about my employment situation. Many of the patrons at the tennis club of my employment, would approach me daily with tennis industry questions. Many were looking for explanations about changing product technology. Particularly, tennis racket technology. I thought," How difficult could it be to have tennis club members and patrons visit my website's Tennis Pro Shop to buy something?" Not too difficult at all. Unless, that; if the patrons could not remember the URL name or the website's domain. I learned that many Internet surfers tend to do quick word searches; they are not too concerned nor do they have the patience to find the exact URL or domain name. For example, if you were to conduct a key-word search for "tennis racquets" Google search results will display 1 – 10 of about 1,810,000 sites for tennis racquets. This first page 1 thru10 of "natural" search or unpaid results are primarily most of my competitors. I needed to know how they got those lead spots...

If I wanted to find the page listing www.TennisAve.com, it would take much more time than I, or anyone else, is willing to spend searching. If I had not registered my website with Google's search engine, or didn't submit my sites to web directories it would be nearly impossible to find my website in the Google search results or any other result pages. I don't know about other website owners, but I desperately wanted to be a part of the World Wide Web boom, boom, boom, sales explosion.

Stand Alone Sites

As I mentioned, many people think the placement of a website on the Internet is the only step to success. However, website owners must take action to generate success.

You have to advertise and market the website's existence in efforts to have visibility. Many website owners become complacent or just do not realize their website is a stand-alone-site. A stand-alone sites in cyberspace are without any neighbors (known as links) or surrounding activity (referred to as traffic). For example, if you open a business or a store in the middle of nowhere, you will not be found. Visitors would need to know your physical address to find you, and they would have to have a very good reason to frequent your store. However, if you market and advertise your business, there is an increased probability you will identify a need for your product and generate traffic to your storefront.

Some stand-alone sites on the Internet are very successful, such as ESPN, Nike, and other well-known companies. But for smaller businesses it is much more difficult and requires more resources to effectively market a stand-alone site. You should aim to have a strong presence on the Internet regardless of what you are promoting; i.e. whether you are selling a service, a product or providing important information. "Virtually every product and service you can think of is selling on the Internet," said Mr. Cute Pants. "It does not matter if 100 or 10,000 other people are selling the same products or service on the Internet," he continued " just as consumers make choices in traditional markets based on price, quality, service, convenience, etc., so do potential buyers on the Internet."

Chapter 2
THE INTERNET

A Brief History of the Internet

Today publishing a website on the Internet is not too difficult. There are so many hosting companies such as, but not limited to Homestead, Intuit, and Hostgator that offer free and/or fee website building packages, free and/or fee hosting and even user friendly merchant accounts. This book provides some basic but important information that you will need to develop success via the Internet after you have published your website. I have made every effort to provide guidelines for you to increase website visibility and presence on the World Wide Web. All in all, this book provides you with quick, inexpensive answers and alternatives on how to promote your website once you have joined (you don't need to purchase six websites) the online world. If you want to take advantage of this exploding market potential, you will have to build a stronger Internet presence for your website using some of the tools I've provided for you.

The Internet 1950 - 1969

The Internet's history dates back to the late 1950's when the U.S. Department of Defense (''DOD'') designed a network of computers to link our many military installations. My boyfriend initially informed me of this and thereafter, he told me my cell phone was tapped. He also said the DOD was listening to all my cell phone conversation and that I should be careful about what I say. Implying that my phone conversations had had top-secret information that the DOD found interested enough to monitor. Although it was a bit flattering to think that the DOD were ease dropping on me, the most interesting response I could muster up was, "Really?" I am, however, cautious of how many times I say "really" because if my mom is tired of hearing that response, I must be driving the DOD personnel crazy!

The fact is, it turns out that back in the late 60's the U.S. Department of Defense developed a network with the sole purpose of connecting several universities, military and defense contractors whom were working jointly on research projects. Additional research and development models that would describe how to connect other types of networks, were designed and resulted in the "Internet" as we know it today.

1970 - 1980

In the 1970's, networking tools such as, The National Center for Supercomputing Applications ("NCSA"), developed the telnet application for remote login, making it easier to connect to a remote computer; later FTP (a file transfer protocol), which standardized the transfer of files between networked computers, appeared. During the 1980's we saw the first desktop computer.

The personal computer revolution continued throughout the 1980's, making access to computer resources and networked information increasingly available to the general public.

The National Science Foundation ("NSF") connected the nation's six supercomputing centers together. This network was called the NSFNET, or NSFNET backbone. Merit Network, Inc. collaborated with International Business Machines Corporation (IBM) and MCI Telecommunications Corporation (MCI) to research and develop faster networking technologies, prompting Al Gore, (U.S. Senator from Tennessee at that time) to popularize the phase "information superhighway". By 1988, Prodigy Service Corp. (online service) began marketing their online database information and networking service. Prodigy offered low-cost set-up software and 2400 baud modem priced at $24.95, opening the network up to commercial interests.

1990 - 2000

Although the basic applications and guidelines that made the Internet possible had existed for almost two decades, the network did not gain a public face until the 1990s. On August 6, 1991 The European Organization for Nuclear Research ("CERN"), a pan-European organization for atomic particle research, publicized a new World Wide Web ("WWW"). English scientist Tim Berners-Lee invented the Web in1989.

The terms Internet and World Wide Web are often used in everyday speech without much distinction. However, the Internet and the WWW are not one and the same.

The Internet is a global data communications system, which is made up of hardware and software infrastructures that provides connectivity between computers. In contrast, the WWW, the web is one of the services communicated via the Internet. It is a collection of interconnected documents and other resources, linked by hyperlinks and URL's.

In 1997, Netscape Navigator 4.0 and Microsoft Internet Explorer 4.0 browser software was released, allowing the widespread use of dynamic web design scripting such as JavaScript and Dynamic Hyper Test (dHTML) to better enhance web pages.

The number of online user's worldwide was estimated at between 60 - 80 million. The development continued and in 1998 the introduction of faster processing hardware helped to drastically lower the price of Personal Computer's as hardware developers shouted for increased market share, thus widening the Internet community even further. In

2000, the number of online users was estimated at 80 – 120 million worldwide, while business entities on the Web exceeded the 500,000 mark.

Present

The Internet, also known as "The Net" has had a greater impact on day-to-day living than that of the home computer, credit cards and even television. Using various statistics, American Domestic Measure (ADM) estimates the population of Internet users to be 1.5 billion as of January 2009.

Regardless of the actual numbers, everyone agrees that the Internet is clearly the single fastest growing business marketplace ever experienced in the entire history of the world. With numbers like this; and growing, the Internet has the power to transform a local company into a global entity instantaneously. Wonderful opportunities exist for small businesses, entrepreneurs and larger companies in cyberspace (The Net).

Many of us use the Internet daily for instant access to things such as online banking, educational services, social networking, live and recorded entertainment, photos, and telephone service.

Personally helping my 7th grader with his homework via the Internet has been priceless. As the Internet continues to transform the processes of shopping, retailing and manufacturing, more consumers, companies and entrepreneurs are realizing the benefits and advantages of e-commerce.

I learned a lot about the Internet with my purchase of six websites. As I went along to publish them, I documented the process as I progress.

THE INTERNET

This book developed as I venture to find the answer to the important question such as, how do people find my websites on the Internet? How do I convert "hits" or visitor to my sites into sales? Most importantly, how do I get my websites to achieve first page results in the search engines and web directories?

Chapter 3
SEARCH ENGINE

Search Engines and Web Directories

Keep in mind the main aim of every Internet business is to achieve good visibility. Making an impression in the vast expanse of the World Wide Web requires registering and/or submitting your website with dozen of indexing systems called "search engines." The process of submitting website details in order to be listed in a web directory is known as directory submission.

All the power that is built into the Internet would be nearly useless if it weren't for the existence of a wide variety of "search engines" such as, Google, Yahoo and Bing (formally MSN). Search engines are programs developed to help you find specific information from among all of the information files and sources on the Internet. Search engines have two basic functions.

1. To go through the information files, word by word, and build an index of the words it finds.
2. To accept "Keywords" that are typed into the search engine by a user trying to locate information containing the specific Keyword requested.

To provide better results to their users, search engines had to adapt to ensure their results pages showed the most relevant search results, rather than unrelated pages stuffed with numerous keywords by unscrupulous webmasters, website owners and in my opinion, some search engine optimizers. Since the success and popularity of a search engine is determined by its ability to produce the most relevant results to any given search, allowing those results to be false would turn users away to other search sources.

1-SEO WANTED

Typically the earlier a website appears in the search engine results page (SERP), the more visitors it will receive from the search engine. Building links from quality online search engines and web directories is an important element of off-page marketing that will help you increase your website's visibility on the Internet.

Examples of well known, general, web directories are Yahoo! Directory and the Open Directory Project (ODP and/or DMOZ). The ODP is the first directory I'm suggesting you submit your website. It's significant is due to its extensive categorization and large number of listings and its free availability for use by other directories and search engines

Please note, a web directory is not a search engine and does not display lists of web pages based on keywords; instead, it lists websites by category and subcategory. Similar to a telephone index or yellow pages that contain lists of people or businesses of a particular area, usually listed alphabetically. Similarly on the Internet, you could find several kinds of 'web' or 'online' directories. The categorization is usually based on the whole website rather than one page or a set of keywords, and sites are often limited to inclusion in only a few categories. Not all websites on the Internet are listed in web directories just as not all businesses are listed in the yellow pages. Web directories often allow site owners to directly submit their site for inclusion, and have editors review submissions for proper form.

There are also some niche directories which focus on restricted regions, single languages, or specialist sectors. One type of niche directory with a large number of sites in existence is the shopping directory. The shopping directories specialize in the listing of retail e-commerce sites. If you sell a product, you definitely want to submit and/or register with shopping directories.

A Small Investment

The following is a list of seven established search engines and web directories on the Internet today:

- http://DMOZ.com   Free
- http://www.Yahoo.com $299 annually
- http://www.Google.com   Free
- http://Bestoftheweb.com $99.95 annually
- http://www.business.com $299 annually
- http://www.Goguides.com $69.95
- http://www.Joeant.com $39.99

The search engines and web directories listed above nets a website its first "authority" links. It is also the fastest way for search engines to find and index pages. They are listed in order of importance.

When submitting to web directories you should always get listed in more than one category. You may want to check the SERPs for keywords and see if your competitor pages have links from these directories. If they do, you may want to make a small investment in these general directories.

Search Engine Marketing Tools

Before you begin the task of submitting and registering your website to search engines and web directories, I think it is crucial to develop an understanding of how powerful they are as a marketing tool, and why you should want to become familiar with how to submit a new (or old) website with each search engine and web directory for yourself. There is no cost to submit with many of the search engines and web directories from the compiled list presented in chapter eight, and it is best to submit your websites to as many of them as possible.

1-SEO WANTED

Search engines are the primary way for Internet users and consumers to find what they are looking for. The search engine purpose is to try to bring organization and efficiency to a chaotic Internet. And it's working! The value they bring to the websites that are found by using them is beyond measure.

Suppose I want to know how 1seowanted.com placed in the top 20 Search Engine Result Pages? In addition, when an Internet user keys in the URL www.1seowanted.com into their search browser, how does 1seowanted.com homepage go directly to their browser or more often than not, the Internet user is directed to other companies offering similar products. Why? The Search engines!

Registering and/or submitting your websites with search engines and web directories facilitate the finding of the new website or older websites for Internet users. When a visitor goes to one of the search engines and/or web directories that your website is registered with, and types in a keyword—either a type of product or service, or a name—that matches any part of your website, the website is found in the search. This allows for more visitors to find your website, which increases traffic and potential business.

You Can Do It Yourself

For online businesses as well as those businesses that depend a lot on their websites for profits, such as, Colonlove.com and TennisAve.com, attracting relevant customers to their websites is imperative. Joya and I now had to find ways to achieve a return on investment and make a profit. To achieve these goals, our websites had to get a conversion rate of 2% or higher at point-of-sale. "Simple math," I could still hear Mr. Cute Pants in my head today, "All you will need is 100 "unique visitors" per month to generate two orders." He said. "Unique visitors are not just Internet surfers on their surfboards they have their wallets in their wetsuits ready to purchase your products."

SEARCH ENGINE

Out of a 100 surfers riding the Internet wave each month, a website getting 2 surfers to buy a product/service, could utter the word, "s-u-c-c-e-s-s-f-u-l."

This requires that a website is designed with due care to ensure that your site is search engine optimized. Though it is possible to design a site yourself, it may not be the easiest thing to bring in the expected results if you are not aware of the different techniques used for search engine optimization.

Remember, keywords are really important if you plan on achieving high search engine rankings. Other aspects that hold as much importance would be the title, the first paragraph of your content and the meta tags. In TennisAve's first year, TennisAve.com had some Internet surfers, mostly from faithful friends, loving relatives and SEOs who visited the website perhaps just to make sure I really had one (I told you it will be cool to have a website), then they would exit. But the Search Engine Optimization consultants would not go a way. Every other day I received a phone call, some nice and some not so nice.

Three years after my throwing the TennisAve.com website up on the Internet, crossing my fingers and waiting, the SEOs not only continued visiting my website but took it upon themselves to do an analysis of my keywords, meta tags and over-all design, then telephoned me, Again! Offering me ways they could help my site achieve web presence and increased sales. To me, a "visitor" is a "visitor" and SEO were not a part of my family and friends plan. If you build it they'll come, the SEO found my website without my asking them, so I had high hopes of continuing my website efforts. So, I built two more websites storefronts. Remember, we did not mirror sites and had no more money to invest in Search Engine Marketing ($3,600). So, Joyas' Salonlist.com was strapped to build www. Colonlove.com and collaborations with my younger sisters Maureen, produced www.1seowanted.com, tripling our cyberspace, space! I vowed "not to spend another penny on this Internet business, until I got a ROI!"

Again, there are potentially 1.5 billion Internet users surfing the net worldwide 24 hours a day/ 7 days a week, which tells me that a website or better yet three websites should have far more visitors to their website(s) than just the 100 or 200 friends and family they ask to visit.

Right about now you're probably thinking, "Boy! Getting my website search engine ready is pretty difficult?" However, it is actually very simple as long as you are able to find your targeted audience (the people who would most likely buy your products.) Now that your website is live, it is time you work on the keywords and the content to introduce your website to the search engines and web directories.

Understand that search engine optimization is a simple form of inbound marketing and it is a way to draw in newly found traffic. The same principles apply as they would in traditional off-line marketing. It is all about being visible in search results or wherever your target audience is grouping such as, web directories, social media groups and niche websites. Begin simple, get your website first-rate and optimized and fully loaded with creative content your audience will enjoy reading.

In a nutshell, that is what search engine optimizers are being paid to do. If your website ranks poorly in the search engines, all your time and effort taken to have your website go live would go in vain. It's your decision! You can hire a Search Engine Optimization experts, or Do-it yourself! It must get done! Either way, it is crucial to your business' success to get it done!

Keywords

The appropriate use of keywords can be a deciding factor to get you a high page ranking. So I want you to prepare a list of 40-50 keywords that best describe your website and the company and products/services you offer. Tip: Find your keywords with the Free Keyword Suggestion Tool from Wordtracker. (**http://freekeywords.wordtracker.com**)

Enter a word for the tool to base its suggestions, and you will get back around 100 options. Once completed, placing them appropriately in your web pages is of equal importance. You should develop a keyword-rich website. Having keywords in the beginning of the content is useful, as the search engine spiders search from the top to down. If it finds the use of the keyword in the very beginning, it means that the site has what it is trying to find. These keywords are words that customers would use when searching for a product/service that your website may offer.

Keyword Phrase

In terms of keywords, you never know what's out there— the ingredient to search engine success could be just a word combination or two away. Tip: The Free keyword Phrase List Generator can help do this. At (**http://tools.seobook.com/keyword-list/generator.php**) follow the directions—this generator is a little more involved than most and you'll wind up with quite a selection of key phrases. Pick carefully to optimize your on line web presence.

Keyword Density

Along with the placement of the keywords and keyword phrases, the keyword density must also be tracked. Ensure that your content contains enough keywords! Having too many will turn off readers; having too few will hurt your search engines rankings. Tip: Achieve the right balance by using the keyword density checker. (**http://www.webconfs.com/keyword-density-checker.php**) There could be sites, which expect the density to be 3% or some favor 5% or 7%. With some research, you will find out the right density to help you earn a higher rank.

Title Tag

The title tag will be checked for keywords by search engine spiders. It is important that your title is written in a creative manner, keeping in mind to use the strongest keywords and keyword phrases. If the title tag has the same keywords used, then it means that the website is relevant to the search. Some search engines place greater importance on the words in your websites title than those within your site.

Alt Tags

Images are used to enhance the look of a website. However, some text browsers do not display images and for such browsers having an Alt Tag proves useful. This tag provides information as to the relevance of an image. Using only the extremely relevant words and keywords helps, rather than too much information, which may lead to the sites elimination or even a ban.

Content Rich and Attractive Design

A website has to be rich in keyword and rich in content as well as attractively designed. Use of keywords and unique content in cliché areas can help to get a high-ranking and increase traffic. Creative content in the body text of the home page, you, once again, want to use your most important keywords and keyword phrases—especially using them in your page headers.

EXTREMELY IMPORTANT: When submitting your website to search engines and directories, do not pepper the title and description of your submission with keywords; do not include lists of any sort in your title and description. Submissions with keyword-stuffed titles or descriptions will be deleted instantly.

Don't worry too much about the process for now. I once read that people remember 10% of what they hear, 50% of what they see, and 90% of what they do. I have included detail step-by-step- instructions, using the Open Directory Project official website's submissions form as my model in chapter seven. If you are not convinced that you can do-it-yourself, I will walk you through the process. I feel SEO is an important part of doing business on the Internet. By visiting my websites 1seowanted.com or TennisAve.com, you can contact me for assistances, for a fee of course. I will be more than happy to help you with the keywords and content of your website as well as the implementation of the submissions process.

It is my hope that this book serves as the perfect guide for many of you who would enjoy optimizing your websites for yourself. Submitting websites with search engines and web directories is one of the first steps an on line business should take when beginning to market its website, not only would it prove to be cost-effective in such a difficult economical environment, but it is not hard to do. In fact, once you put all the optimizing aspect together, you will dramatically increase your reach, sales and profits! Best of all it's fun!

Chapter 4
SEARCH ENGINE OPTIMIZATION

A Brief History of Search Engine Optimization

To be honest, the constant solicitation from Search Engine Optimization (SEO) personnel was the basis for my education in its meaning and value. The first year of purchasing our websites, Joya and I were bombarded with phone calls from SEOs talking about the important of marketing the websites we now owned and how they could help to make it happen for a hefty fee, more money! It seemed to me that the SEOs needed me more than I needed them to increase traffic to my website. Six years later, I continue my anger toward Mr. Cute Pants for failing to mention SEO, its value, implementation cost and his company's affiliation with some of the SEO providers.

Wikipedia defines search engine optimization, or SEO, as the process of improving the volume of quality of traffic to a website or a web page from search engines via "natural" or un-paid ("organic" or "algorithmic") search result as opposed to other forms of search engine marketing (SEM) which may deal with paid inclusion.

The SEO process is twofold:

1. Internal improvement of each website page located in the backoffice to include keywords frequency, keyword phrases, meta tags, headings, and links and,

2. External enhancement through factors like, PageRank, backlinks and hyperlinks.

1-SEO WANTED

The acronym "SEO" can refer to "search engine optimizers," a term adopted by an industry of consultants who carry out optimization projects on behalf of clients, and by employees who perform SEO services in-house. As an Internet marketing strategy, SEO considers how search engines work and what words used in a person's search.

Optimizing a website primarily involves editing its content and HTML coding to both increase its relevance to specific keywords and to remove barriers to the indexing activities of search engines. Search engine optimizers may offer SEO as a stand-alone service or as a part of a broader marketing campaign. Since effective SEO may require changes to the HTML source code of a site, SEO tactics may be incorporated into website development and design. The term "search engine friendly" (see appendix 1) may be used to describe website designs, menus, content management systems and shopping carts that are easy to optimize.

The actual term "search engine optimization" was coined around 1997. But even before that, in the early days of Yahoo!, people were already beginning to work with SEO concepts by testing out different keywords, keyword densities and/or website pages placement.

The Early Years

In the early days of search engines, webmasters (owner of a website) and/or content providers would only need to submit their page addresses or URLs to a given search engines, which would then send "spiders" to crawl through and index the sites. As soon as people started to realize the value of having their websites show up on page one of search engine's results pages, they began looking for ways to manipulate the search engine's indexing algorithms to increase their website's PageRank (see chapter 6) and frequency.

SEARCH ENGINE OPTIMIZATION

Initially, search algorithms relied on on-site information to determine page rankings. In other words, they were depended upon information that was provided by the webmasters; Such as, keyword density, meta tags and index files. All anyone needed to do was enter in the right keywords and keyword phases in an adequate density, and they would start to see front-page search engine rankings in no-time. Some SEO started manipulating HTML source attributes to get their clients higher rankings. This caused the search engine's results to become unreliable, often filled with spam pages whose keyword tags did not accurately represent the pages' actual content. The first algorithm "crackers" appeared around 1997. By decoding a search engine's ranking algorithm, which at the time was easier than Rubik's Cube, a dishonest webmaster could send websites into the top 10 results at will. 1997 was that same year, when several SEO providers were able to decode all 35 parameters of Excite's ranking algorithm.

The Arrival of Google

Search engines recognized that webmasters and SEOs were making efforts to achieve high rank in their search results' pages, and that some webmasters and SEOs were even manipulating their rankings in search results by stuffing pages with excessive or irrelevant keywords. This had gotten the search engines in trouble. Search engines are the primary way for Internet users to find what they are looking for; therefore these search engines had to find another method of ranking pages that would actually reflect a page's value and searched relevance. Early search engines, such as Infoseek, adjusted their algorithms in an effort to prevent webmasters from manipulating rankings. More complex algorithms were being developed that took into account several off-site factors. For example link popularity and directory age became important ranking determinants, while cracking search engine algorithms became a much more difficult and sophisticated task.

At this point, Alta Vista seem to be the most popular and comprehensive, the rest of Internet users were evenly split between Lycos, Yahoo!, MSN, and InfoSeek. Despite the improved algorithms, "black hat" SEOs were still able to find ways to manipulate them; and "page- jacking" and website theft was rampant.

Google is a company founded on September 4, 1998, by Stanford University graduate students, Larry Page and Sergey Brin. Google's algorithm, named PageRank (see chapter 6), determined site rankings by measuring the quantity and quality of their inbound links. Google's superior, relevant search results immediately attracted a loyal following, and competing search engines started to realize the importance of keeping up with Google's new page ranking methodology.

As the new millennium approached, Google solidified its spot as the authentic engine, while engines like Infoseek were becoming part of SEO themselves and/or Internet history. By 2001, users had abandoned such other search engines as Lycos, Excite, AltaVista and Hotbot.

The Google Age

By 2004, three major search engines were being used; Google, MSN and Yahoo! Each began to incorporate undisclosed page ranking factors into their ranking algorithms. The era of keyword-spamming SEO had ended. SEO techniques are now classified into two broad categories: techniques that search engines recommend as part of good design, and those techniques that search engines do not approve.

Search engines attempt to minimize the effect of the latter, among them spamdexing. Methods such as link farms and keywords stuffing, that degrades both the relevance of search results and the user-experience are abhorred. Some industry commentators have classified these methods, and the practitioners who employ them, as either "white hat" SEO, or "black hat" SEO.

White hats tend to produce results that last a long time, whereas black hats anticipate that their sites may eventually be banned (mirroring), either temporarily or permanently once the search engines discover what they are doing. Search engines also look for sites that employ these techniques in order to remove them from their indices. Webmasters and SEOs have to rely on more creative ways to promote content and generate inbound links in order to achieve long-term website presence.

In 2005, Google starts personalizing search results by taking into account a user's search history to develop customized results pages whenever that user is logged in. In 2007, Google started a campaign against paid links affecting PageRank. In 2009, the Company announces it will attempt to stop the effects of PageRank "sculpting" that come as a result of no-follow links.

Today, SEO is for the most part, a conversation with Google Search. Due to the high marketing value of targeted search results, there is potential for an adversarial relationship between search engines and SEOs.

In 2005, an annual conference, AIRWeb, (Adversarial Information Retrieval on the Web), was created to discuss and minimize the damaging effects of overly aggressive web content providers. Some search engines have also reached out to the SEO industry and are frequent sponsors and guests at SEO conferences, chats, and seminars. In fact, with the advent of paid inclusion, some search engines now have a vested interest in the health of the optimization community.

1-SEO WANTED

Google has over 70% of today's search engine users and is thus the place you have to be in order to start driving "natural" traffic to your website. SEO campaigns are much more laborious and complex now than they were a decade ago, but this is largely a good thing. Users get better and more relevant results, while webmasters and content providers must provide real value if creating high rank status on search results' pages.

Major search engines provide information and guidelines that help webmasters with site optimization. Google has a Sitemaps program that helps webmasters learn if search engines are having any problems indexing their website and also provides data on Google traffic to the website. It is free. Yahoo! Site Explorer provides a way for webmasters to submit URLs, determine how many pages are in the Yahoo! index and view link information. There are many resources if you're the do-it-yourself type. This information will be vital when creating SEO for your website's presence. In the next chapter, I introduce the Pros and Cons of hiring your own SEOs.

Chapter 5
HIRE A SEARCH ENGINE
OPTIMIZER

Hire a good SEOs

Don't over think it—SEO is simply marketing. I had a tendency to over think SEO at first. Then I started to realize that I needed SEO and I learned of the implementation cost. SEO is not a magic pill or a secret potion; it is simply a different type of marketing approach to get Internet traffic to find your website. One reason why I was receiving so many phone calls from the SEO's, was because they knew SEO is not going away. Keep in mind that SEO is new and fresh and it is going through many various changes but it is an important concept to take hold of sooner than later.

SEO is not rocket science. It requires putting up new content on your website to those pages that contain the most importance information about your business, along with writing new custom meta text for those particular pages. If you are limited on time but have unlimited resources to hire a good SEO, here are the Pros and Cons of hiring a good SEO to fully optimize your website in order to drive traffic to it.

Without a doubt, a website without traffic cannot succeed! If you hire a SEO, you are making a big decision that can potentially improve your site and save time, but you can also risk damage to your site and reputation. Make sure you understand the potential advantages, as well as the disadvantages that an irresponsible SEOs can do to your website business.

1-SEO WANTED

Not all SEO's are created equal. If one person takes one path that doesn't necessarily mean that all the others will take that same path. SEO come with vastly different experiences and knowledge levels, so comparing oranges to oranges in the Internet marketing industry can often times be difficult. SEO companies that employ overly aggressive techniques can get their clients websites banned from the search engine results. For example, in 2005, I read that the Wall Street Journal reported on a company, Traffic Power, which allegedly used high-risk techniques and failed to disclose those risks to its clients. Wired magazine reported that the same Company sued a blogger and SEO, for writing about the ban. Google's Matt Cutts later confirmed that Google did, in fact, ban the company and some of its clients. Go ahead, Google it, "Traffic Power" to read more.

It is up to you to figure out if SEO is the right pathway to help you with your online business goals. Make sure you hire an SEO in the early process stages of site redesign, that way you and your SEOs can ensure that your site is designed to be Search Engine-friendly. Don't panic if you have already launched a site, a good SEO can also help improve an existing site.

Who Can You Trust?

Remember that most SEOs offer unique traits and skills that have been acquired over time through practice and patience. Some useful services that SEOs provide include:

- Review of your website content or structure
- Technical advice on website development: Hosting, re-directs, error pages, use of JavaScript, etc.
- Content development
- Management of online business development campaigns
- Keyword research

- Expertise in specific markets and geographies.

You have to probe and ask questions that can help you determine the right SEO such as:

- Can you show examples of previous work and share some success stories?
- Do you follow the Google Webmaster Guidelines?
- Do you offer any online marketing services or advice to compliment your "natural" search business?
- What kind of results could a website owner expect to see, and in what time frame?
- How do websites measure success?
- What is your experience in my industry?
- What are your most significant SEO techniques?
- How long have you been in business, and can I have your website address and references?
- How can I expect to communicate with you? Will you share with me all the changes you make to my site, and provide detailed information about your recommendations and the reasoning behind them?

Beware

While you consider whether to go with an SEO consultant, you may want to do some more research on the industry. Beware of SEOs that claim to guarantee rankings, allege a "special relationship" with the top search engines, or advertise a "priority submit" to them.

These were the not so nice telephone calls I spoke of earlier, more like telemarketers refusing to let me off the phone.

There is no priority submission for many search engines. In fact, the only way you can get listed on search engines is to submit a site through the "Add URL" which you can do yourself for free, it will only cost you time and effort.

Remember the adage there are no stupid questions and don't be afraid to ask for explanations, if something is unclear. If SEOs create deceptive or misleading content on your behalf, such as doorway pages or "throwaway" domains, your site could be removed entirely from search engine index, if this happens, you are responsible for the actions of any companies you hire, so it's best to be sure you know exactly how they intend to "help" you.

2010 Marketing Workshop

At an Internet workshop conference that I recently attended (I received a MP3 player at this workshop) I was surprise and disappointed to hear that the cost of websites had dropped from $1,400 in 2004 to $199 in 2010.

However, the sales pitch was revolutionized from websites production to search engine marketing (SEM) of website produced. Remember, SEM is when the optimization of a website uses payment to be included in a search engine. For example, sponsor links. The ones you see on the right side of the search pages could run you into the poor house if you are a newbie one-woman-operation such as I. While SEO certainly existed at the 2005 Internet workshop that I had attended, it was not discussed.

The 2010, Internet marketing workshop began with SEO and end with SEM, for a very hefty fee of $3,600. Be sure to understand where your money goes. Some SEOs will promise to rank you highly in search engines, but place you in the advertising section rather than in the search results.

A few SEOs will even change their bid prices in real time to create the illusion that they "control" other search engines and can place themselves in the slot of their choice. I like the Google search engine results pages (SERPs) because the advertisements is clearly labeled with sponsor links (paid inclusion) and separated from the free search results, on the right side of the page, but be sure to ask any SEO you're considering which fees go toward permanent inclusion and which apply toward temporary advertising.

Website Abuser

One common scam is the creation of "shadow" domains that funnel users to a site by using deceptive redirects. For example, you key in a URL such as tennisave.com then your directed to an entirely different URL such as bad-baby.com. These shadow domains often will be owned by the SEO who claims to be working on your behalf.

However, if the relationship sours, the SEO may point the domain to a different site, or even to a competitor's domain. If that happens, you are paying to develop a competing site owned entirely by the SEO. This happened to my younger sister when she decided to go with a different SEM company for her website. I believe she did and you can report this with the Federal Trade Commission FTC. (See page 36)

Another illicit practice is to place "doorway" pages loaded with key-words on the client's site somewhere. The SEO promises this will make the page more relevant for more queries. This is inherently false since individual pages are rarely relevant for a wide range of key-words. More sinister, however, is that these doorway pages often con-tain hidden links to the SEO's other clients as well. Such doorway pages drain away the link popularity of a site and route it to the SEO and its other clients, which may include sites with unsavory or illegal content.

There are a few warning signs that you may be dealing with a scoun-drel SEO. It's far from a comprehensive list, so if you have any doubts, you should trust your instincts. By all means, feel free to walk in another direction if the SEO:

- owns shadow domains, just ask them!
- puts links to their other clients on doorway pages
- offers to sell keywords in the address bar
- doesn't distinguish between actual search results and ads that appear on search results pages
- guarantees ranking, but only on obscure, long keyword phrases you would get anyway
- operates with multiple aliases or falsified WHOIS info
- gets traffic from "fake" search engines, spyware, or scumware
- has had domains removed from index or is not itself listed in the major leading search engines
- requests your FTP account information or root access to your server

Remember, if you feel that you were deceived by an SEO in any way, you may want to report it. Try to get a back-up file of the title of your business, description and keywords used to promote your web- site on the Internet while you are working with this SEO. This information will service as a starting point for you to begin registering and submitting to the search engines and web directories for yourself.

In the United States, the Federal Trade Commission (FTC) handles complaints about deceptive or unfair business practices. To file a complaint, visit: http://www.ftc.gov/ and click on "File a Complaint Online," call 1-877-FTC-HELP, or write to:

Federal Trade Commission
CRC-240
Washington, D.C. 20580

Chapter 6
PAGERANK

What is PageRank?

PageRank ("PR") is a link analysis algorithm used by the Google Internet search engine that assigns a numerical weighting to each element of a hyperlinked set of documents, such as WWW with the purpose of "measuring" its relative importance within the set. The algorithm may be applied to any collection of entities with reciprocal quotations and references (see the graph on following page). The numerical weight that it assigns to any given website (E) is also called the PageRank of the website (E)) and denoted by PR (E). The number calculated by the algorithm or the Pagerank, is a function of the quantity and strength of inbound links.

PageRank was developed at Stanford University by Larry Page (it is named after him) and Sergey Brin; as part of a research project about a new kind of search engine. Larry Page and Sergey Brin were graduate students at Stanford University, who developed the search engine that relied on a mathematical algorithm to rate the prominence of web pages called "backrub."

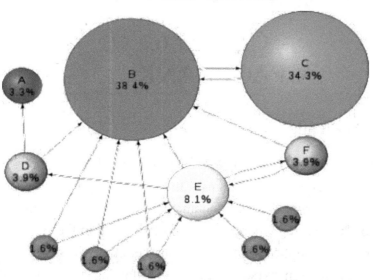

Mathematical Page Ranks (out of 100) for a simple network (Page Ranks reported by Google are rescaled logarithmically) Page C has a higher Page Rank than Page E, even though it has fewer links to it: the link it has is much higher valued. A web surfer who chooses a random link on every page (but with 15% likelihood jumps to a random page on the whole web) is going to be on Page E for 8.1% of the time. (The 15% likelihood of jumping to an arbitrary page corresponds to a damping factor of 85%) Without damping, all web surfers would eventually end up on Pages A, B, or C, and all other pages would have Page Rank zero. Page A is assumed to link to all pages in the web, because it has no outgoing links.

The raw equation looks something like this: $PR(A)=(1-d)+d(PR(T1)/C(T1)+...+PR(Tn)/C(Tn))$

Techy stuff, I know, or do I? ...

Google Describes PageRank

Google describes PageRank as "PageRank reflects our view of the importance of web pages by considering more than 500 million variables and 2 billion terms. Pages that we believe are important pages receive a higher PageRank and are more likely to appear at the top of the search results.

PageRank also considers the importance of each page that casts a vote, as votes from some pages are considered to have greater value, thus giving the linked page greater value. We have always taken a pragmatic approach to help improve search quality and create useful products, and our technology uses the collective intelligence of the web to determine a page's importance."

In essence, Google interprets my incoming link from TennisAve.com PR1 to Colonlove.com PR3 as a vote, by TennisAve.com, for Colonlove.com. A web page gains PageRank by receiving inbound links from other pages; a web page gives PageRank by linking to other pages. But, Google says it looks at more than the sheer volume of votes, or links that a page receives; it also analyzes the PageRank of the page that casts the vote. Votes cast by pages that are themselves "important" weigh more heavily and help to make other pages "important." Links into a site cannot harm a site, but links from a site can be harmful, so be careful which sites you link to. If a site has a PR0, it is usually a penalty and it would be unwise to link to it. Remember! Google ranks Web Pages not Websites.

Inbound and outbound links

Does anyone know what the probability of a PageRank 0 is? You follow me? I learned, the phase "You follow me?" from my older sisters, Andrea. She does not usually mean for me to literally follow her around, however, I do hope that you follow me here! Let's look closer at PageRank resulting from a "ballot" among all the other pages on the World Wide Web about how important a web page is. A hyperlink to a page counts as a vote of support. The PageRank of a page is defined recursively and depends on the number and PageRank metric of all pages that link to it ("incoming links"). For example, Oprah.com has a PR7 in the Google toolbar (directions on how to check Google PR follows), don't feel too proud to ask her for a link, if need be. Please! Oprah, please!

If TennisAve.com receives a link from Oprah.com and other web pages with higher PageRank, TennisAve.com page increases up in PageRank. In other words, Tennisve.com could move from PR1 to PR2 on the Google toolbar meter by receiving just one link from a very important website such as, Oprah.com. If there are no links to a web page, there is no support for that page. Don't worry, Oprah's web page does not lose PageRank by linking to my poorly ranked web page, she just passes rank on. The value of past on PageRank is divided by the number of existing outbound links on the linking web page. Due to the damping factor, the amount of PageRank a page receives from an inbound link is limited to 85% of the total value that leaves the linking web page. Again, there is no need in getting into the techy stuff. Just know you can increase PageRank with inbound links from different domains by optimizing your website's on-page and off-page structure.

What is your websites PR?

As I began to submit my website to search engines and web directories for increasing TennisAve.com's visibility, I sent an email to a tennis resort website asking for a reciprocal link. The resort replied with an email that read, "Dear TennisAve.com, when you get a Page Rank of 4 or better write us back." I wondered how the tennis resort knew my present PageRank. Then I pondered how I would get my PageRank to 4 or better to attract higher ranked websites. Or, better yet, attract advertisers?

Knowing your web page PageRank is very important. It is also necessary to know the PageRank of other sites because, as I mentioned,

PAGERANK

Google factors the quality of sites that link to yours much more than the quantity of sites that link to yours and, apparently, (like the tennis resort email suggested) other webmasters and/or website owners are considering the same factors.

So keep a watchful eye out for the Oprah dot coms with the higher-ranked sites! A link from Oprah to a website like TennisAve.com is worth more than 100 links from sites with a PR1, or 1000 links from sites with PR0. Make sure you install the PageRank checker or do instant website PR checks for use with your link building campaign.

A Dating Service

Since everyone learns differently, I want to explain the PageRank concept using additional analogies: First, let's think of PageRank as a dating service in cyberspace. The roadmap you use to find and date the prefect man or woman is the same concept you should use during your link building process, when asking for reciprocal links or search engine and web directory submission. On a scale of 1 – 10, you probably want to date someone whom is a 5 or better. In a perfect cyberspace world, you want to date (link) someone whom has status (rank), such as, a doctor PR10, lawyer PR8, skilled worker PR6 etc. These are my opinions of how I would relate working status to Page Rank, not Googles.

Remember, the point is to link up with someone who has excellent status. So, put your knowledge of PR in exploration of an individual that has the highest status (rank). Arrange a date (link) with Mr. PR10 or Miss. PR7, and you will become far more important and happier within this relationship (Internet) than if you did not date (link) at all. On the other hand, if you decide to date (link) Mr.PR0 because he has "Cute Pants" or Miss. PR1 because "she's nice," but whom have the same status (rank) as you or slightly worse you would have to date (link) one thousand Cute Pants or one thousand nice chicks just to nudge the PageRank meter in the right direction.

Expressions of PageRank

The second analogy is mathematical that shows the important of an increase PageRank. The PageRank estimates the likelihood that a given page will be reached by a web user who randomly surfs the web, and follows links from one page to another.

In essence, PageRank is all about the probability distribution used to represent the likelihood that a user will randomly click on links and arrive at any particular web page. The PageRank probability is expressed as a numeric value between 0 and 1. A 0.5 probability is commonly expressed as a "50% chance" of something happening. Hence, a PR 0.7 means that the Oprah page has a 70% chance that a person clicking on a random link will be directed to the Oprah.com page. I have not seen many websites with the PageRank of 100%. Of course, Google has PR10, Yahoo has PR9 and one of my favorite web pages, Wikipedia.com has a PageRank of 8, at the time of this writing.

Be Competitive

Remember, in order to be competitive on "natural" (a.k.a. "organic" or "algorithmic") or un-paid search engines, you need to have a healthy PageRank for the front and/or home page of your website. On the PR scale from 0 to 10 (the maximum) a PR of 40% is generally healthy and competitive. However, competitiveness is relative as it pertains to subject. Some categories require PR5 to remain competitive versus a PR3 for other subjects to compete within an industry. There are always an exception to a rule however, it is best to work on achieving a PR4 or higher over time. Keep in mind that for a commercial website, a PR6 (60%) is probably the maximum achievable

PR. A PR7 (70%) and higher can generally only be achieved through a multi-million dollar public relations campaign.

It has been said that to move from a PR4 to PR5 is more difficult than moving from a PR0 to a PR1. Be patience but persistent.

Free Page Rank checker for your website!

Now, let's take a closer look at the PageRank checker. It is a free tool to check Google page ranking of any website pages easily and to display your site's PageRank value on your web pages. Remember! It is free! I love free...

By adding the page rank checker tool (the icon) to your site you can instantly and easily check web rank of all your website pages right on your website. Go to **https://www.prchecker.info**. In order to install the Page Rank checking tool on your site, you just need to add a small piece of HTML code to those web pages where you want to check the page rank and free PR checker tool will show the small icon that displays the current Google.com PageRank of the web page. » Here is an example of the small icon shown by page rank checker tool that display the Current Google PageRank value of this (https://www.prchecker.info/) web page.

Familiarize yourself with the PR Tool to get an understanding of how PageRank differs from one site to the next. Each time you visit a web page, you can easily view the PageRank of that page. Write down a few of the websites having healthy PageRank relative to their business because you may want to go back and ask them for a reciprocal link at a later date.

The Google PageRank meter displays PageRank as a whole number between 0 and 10. The most popular websites have a PageRank of 10. Google uses a graphical meter, but you can see the actual numerical score by simply submitting the URL of the website, web page or domain name. So, start paying close attention to the PageRank meter!

Don't obsess over PageRank

Many search engine optimizers (those SEOs guys who deal with improving the number and/or quality of visitors to a website from "natural" search engine listing) believe that the Google toolbar PageRank is not of great use. It is often months out of date and does not determine a rank of a web page. So, optimizers say, please do not obsess over the Google PageRank meter. However, in December 2009, Google updated its PageRank meter, and many website owners are now happily reporting increases in PageRank from a 0 to 3, overnight!

I, for one, enjoy following the Google PageRank meter and I feel it does have some value. When the time comes for me to begin building off-page reciprocal links with other webmasters, I will look at their website PageRank and only request linkages with sites that have a PageRank of 4 or better. Also, the PageRank could be used to find out who you believe to be your greatest competitors on the web. Compare your website PageRank to theirs. You may want to set a goal to eventually exceed your competitor's PageRank. Most importantly, I like to know amongst all the other pages I'm visiting on the World Wide Web, just how popular or as Google puts it, how important a page is non-competitively.

The name "PageRank" is a "trademark" of Google. The PageRank process has been patented (U.S. Patent 6,285,999). However, the patent is assigned to Stanford University and not to Google. Google has exclusive license rights on the patent from Stanford University. The university received 1.8 million shares of Google stock in exchange for use of the patent; the shares were sold in 2005 for $336 million.

PAGERANK

There are other link-based ranking algorithms for Web pages including the HITS algorithm invented by Jon Kleinberg (used by Teoma and now Ask.com), the IBM CLEVER project, and the Trust Rank algorithm. In addition, many of these link-based ranking sites have webmasters tools and informational pages that you should become familiar with so that you can decide what may be best for your website.

In practice, the PageRank concept has proven to range from vulnerable to manipulative. Extensive research has been devoted to identifying falsely inflated PageRank and ways to ignore those links. As you have read in the Search Engine and Search Engine Optimization sections of the book, please keep in mind that the rules are always changing and the submissions process is getting tougher. You may not put all of emphasis on the PR but link building is always going to be in the background of the web.

Chapter 7
THE OPEN DIRECTORY PROJECT

"How-To" Make Directory Submissions Yourself

The ODP allows over 400 (estimated) other major websites on the Internet to copy their entire directory. If you submit and are accepted to the ODP, in only a short period of time that link propagates itself onto the other websites that copy the ODP. Your one link really generates 400 links.

Webmasters and/or website owners would first have to submit their website details to a few web directories on the list in order to be listed in at least one, if not all of them. Since most web directories allow sites to be listed in them completely free of cost, it would make business sense to have your website submitted to as many search engine friendly directories (see Appendix 1) as possible. Given these benefits, building links through directories is a decision that every website owner should seriously make.

Colonlove.com

Here is the information (in bold) I used for the submission of Colon-Love.com to the ODP.

- Title: Usually five or six words, e.g. "**Colon Love.com**".
- Write a description of the website that would meet the criteria for each search engine: Find relief for constipation, irritable bowel syndrome, eczema, and related illnesses through colon cleansing. Have a traveling colon hydro-therapist supply a colonic irrigation session in your home, executive suite, health venue or healing circle.

- Your keywords should have between 20- 200 characters. This field may be altogether absent in some directories; however, most directories offer this as an optional field, such as, keyword frequency, meta tags, headings, links and site structure: Keywords: **colon cleanse, colonic irrigation, traveling colon hydro-therapist, chronic constipation, eczema, irritable bowel syndrome.**
- Decide where your site should be categorized in each search engine and directory.
-

It is very important for you to first browse through all the options of categories and sub-categories to find the right category in which to submit your site. Remember that directory links would not be of any use if they come from irrelevant categories that are not related to the theme and content of your site. Hence choice of category is very important. If you do not find a category that is suitable for your website, some directories also offer the option of suggesting a category. If the directory editor approves your suggestion, a new category would be created: **Alternative health.**

- E-mail address: Colonlove@hotmail.com
- Contact name Joya

A small investment of your time today and a few hours a day dedicated to your website will bring you a substantial amount of traffic and, of equal importance, will dramatically improve your website's Internet presence and Google PageRank. Submitting your website to all the important web directories is the foundation of good, do-it-yourself off-page optimization of your website.

Remember, Keywords are the key aspect to each search engine's indexing and usage (3% to 7%). When a business has developed its website, keywords and descriptive information should be high priority, both for spiders to find and use, as well as when submitting and registering with each search engine and web directory. So begin with what you already have, get creative; use the Internet, use your logo, be clear by keeping your website simple but also keep it fresh.

Step-By-Step Open Directory Project

Now let's submit your website to the Open Directory Project at www.dmoz.org. It is one of the most important live directories on the web, and the submission process is straight forward. After you submit your website(s) to the ODP, you will then follow the same procedures for the others search engines and web directories. Use "the list" presented in Chapter eight of this book to begin today!

After you have visited the search engine and the directory home page, your next step would be to submit your website. To do this, you would first need to look for the option in the directory that says 'Add Listing', 'Add URL', 'Submit Site', Submit Link', 'Suggest Site', 'Suggest URL' or 'Suggest Listing'.

These are the common terms that can be found on the home page and category pages of a search engine and/or web directory. The option to add or submit a site is usually found right at the top or at the bottom of the front page. For the ODP, the option is found at the top as Suggest URL: When you click on this "Suggest URL" link, you will be taken through the submission Process.

The Open Directory Project

The Open Directory Project (aka DMOZ or ODP) is a web directory of Internet resources. A web directory is something akin to a huge reference library. The directory is hierarchically arranged by subject from the broad to specific. The ODP is maintained by community editors who evaluate sites for inclusion in their directory. They are the experts, and all submissions are subject to editorial evaluation.

1-SEO WANTED

ODP is not a search engine and they do not take all websites, so please don't take it personally should your site not be accepted. Their goal (like many other directories) is to make the directory as useful as possible for the users, not to have the directory include all (or even most) of the sites that could possibly be listed or serve as a promotional tool for the entities listed.

To keep their directory running smoothly, they have set up policies for submitting sites for their consideration. They may reject, delete, or edit submissions that violate their policies.

You should take a few moments to understand the ODP policies and the steps to submit a site before you begin. Failure to understand and follow these instructions generally will result in the rejection of a submission.

Identify the single best category for your site. The Open Directory has an enormous array of subjects to choose from. You should submit a site to the single most relevant category. Sites submitted to inappropriate or unrelated categories may be rejected or removed.

Note: Some categories do not have "suggest URL" or "update URL" links. These categories don't accept submissions, so you should find a more specific category for your site.

Once you've selected the best category for your site, go directly to that category on dmoz.org and then click "suggest URL." Follow the instructions on the submission form carefully.

Actual Step-by-step submission of TennisAve.com on 2/5/2010:

Submitting my Site to the Open Directory

THE OPEN DIRECTORY PROJECT

ODP thanked me for my interest in the Open Directory Project. Submitting a site is easy, but before I proceeded with my site submission form, they asked that I do two things.

EXAMPLE:

A site on Breast Cancer should be submitted to:

Top: Health: Conditions and Diseases: Cancer : Breast Cancer not

Top: Health: Conditions and Diseases

This is an important distinction in the world of web categorization, and it ensures speedy processing of your site.

---

1. Please take a moment to review some of our submission policies and instructions. It is important that you understand these policies. Failure to understand and follow these policies generally will result in the rejection of a submission.
2. Please check to be sure that this is the single category you think your site should be listed in. The Open Directory has a rich subject tree, and it helps everyone if you search around for the best category. This also helps expedite our review of your site.

Please note: The ODP are not a search engine and pride them self on being highly selective. They don't accept all sites, so "AGAIN" please don't take it personally should your site not be accepted.

Step One:

1-SEO WANTED

Choose the best category that your site should be listed in.

Category: Shopping: Sports: Tennis

*Are you sure this is the most descriptive category for your site? If you are unsure, please take a little extra time in searching the directory and find the most appropriate category.

Site URL	www.Tennisave.com

● ○ ○ ○

What type of link is this? Reg PDF RSS Atom

*URL stands for Uniform Resource Locator, which means your site address. Example: http://dmoz.org

1. Do not add mirror sites.

2. Do not submit an URL that contains only the same or similar content as other sites you may have listed in the directory. Multiple submissions of the same or related sites may result in the exclusion and/or deletion of those and all affiliated sites.

3. Do not disguise your submission and submit the same URL more than once. Example: http://www.dmoz.org and http://www.dmoz.org/index.html.

4. Do not submit any site with an address that redirects to another address.

5. The Open Directory has a policy against the inclusion of sites with illegal content. Examples of illegal material include child pornography; libel; material that infringes any intellectual property right; and material that specifically advocates, solicits or abets illegal activity (such as fraud or violence).

6. Do not submit sites "under construction."
7. Submit pornographic sites to the appropriate category under Adult.
8. Submit non-English sites to the appropriate category under World.
9. Don't submit sites consisting largely of affiliate links.

Title of Site: | Tennis Avenue |

*Please supply a short and descriptive title.

- Always opt for the official name of the site.
- Do not use ALL CAPITAL letters.
- Exclude promotional language in the title.

Site Description

> The information and sports store, specializing in tennis products. Offering the perfect selection of tennis racquets, tennis equipment, tennis balls, ball machines, strings, backpacks, tennis apparel, tips, lessons instructions and much more.

*Keep the description of your site brief - no longer than 25-30 words. A well-written, objective description will make listing your website easier.

- Do not use any HTML tags
- Write in complete sentences and/or descriptive phrases using proper grammar, punctuation and correct spelling.
- Do not use ALLCAPS in your description.

- Avoid capitalizing every word in a sentence.
- Don't repeat the title of your site in the description.
- Avoid using promotional language and strings of key words and search terms. Words and phrases like "cool" and "best darn site" will be removed.

Your E-mail Address:

Marymboston@aol.com

SA7688S5

User* Please verify the text in the image. The text in the image and the **Verification:** text you submit in the input field must match.

Can't read this text?

Get New Text

SA7 688S5

Can't see this image?

Play Audio

Submission Agreement

In exchange for ODP's consideration of the website I am submitting, I agree

o To be bound by the ODP's Terms of Use.

○   To waive any claim related to the inclusion, placement, exclusion, or removal of this or any other site in the ODP Directory or to the title or description of any site appearing in the ODP Directory; and

○   To grant Netscape Communications Corporation a non-exclusive, royalty-free license to use, publish, copy, edit, modify, or create derivative works from my submission.

I also acknowledge that Netscape and the ODP have unfettered editorial discretion to determine the structure and content of the directory and that, because a site's placement in the directory is subject to change or deletion at any time, I may not rely on any aspect of a site's inclusion in the directory. (i.e. "submission" means the title and descriptive information you supply for your site, not the actual website or its contents).

I have read and understand the submissions guidelines,

Submit

and I'm ready to submit my site

After you click the submit button, you should see the following message.

Submission Received

Your site submission has been received.

An editor will review your submission for inclusion in the directory.

Once your site has been accepted into the Open Directory, it may take anywhere from 2 weeks to several months for your site to be listed on partner sites which use the Open Directory data, such as AOL Search, AltaVista, HotBot, Google, Lycos, Netscape Search, etc. We make updates of the data available weekly, but each partner has their own update schedule.

Procedures after Your Site is submitted:

An ODP editor will review your submission to determine whether to include it in the directory.

Depending on factors such as the volume of submissions to the particular category, it may take several weeks or more before your submission is reviewed. Please only submit a URL to the Open Directory once. Again, multiple submissions of the same or related sites may result in the exclusion and/or deletion of those and all affiliated sites. Disguising your submission and submitting the same URL more than once is not permitted.

Updating Your Site

If a site has been accepted for inclusion in the directory but you are dissatisfied with how the site is described or titled, you may go to the category where it is listed, and fill out the "update URL" form. If you are dissatisfied with the category in which your site is listed, you may send an email to an editor for the category explaining your disagreement. Be polite and civil -- threatening or abusive behavior will not be tolerated.

If (but only if) you are dissatisfied with the editor's response, you may then use the "Feedback" link at the top of the page to "appeal" the editor's decision.

Be specific concerning your disagreement (including why you believe the editor's response is inadequate). Comments made through the feedback link are reviewed by the ODP staff, who will make the final decision. Please do NOT send correspondence to Netscape, as that will only slow down and complicate the process. We take all feedback seriously and give it our thoughtful consideration. But please remember that we must exercise our discretion and make numerous judgment calls as to how to make the ODP as useful as possible -- no matter what decision we make, we may not always satisfy everyone.

Getting Your Site into Portals and Search Engines Using ODP Data

If your site has been accepted into the Open Directory, it may take anywhere from 2 weeks to several months for your site to be listed on partner sites which use the Open Directory data, such as AOL Search, Google, Netscape Search, Yahoo Search, and hundreds of other sites. They make updates of the data available weekly, but each partner has their own update schedule.

Reminder of the ODP Editorial Discretion

Please recognize that making the ODP a useful resource requires us to exercise broad editorial discretion in determining the content and structure of the directory. That discretion extends (but is not limited) to what sites to include, where in the directory sites are placed, whether and when to include more than one link to a site, when deep linking is appropriate, and the content of the title and description of the site. In addition, a site's placement in the directory is subject to change or deletion at any time at our sole discretion. You should not rely on any aspect of a site's inclusion in the directory. Please understand that an editor's exercise of discretion may not always treat all submissions equally. You may not always agree with our choices, but we hope you recognize that we do our best to make fair and reasonable decision.

TennisAve.com was accepted in 2010

Remember! The ODP allows over 400 (estimated) other major web sites on the Internet to copy their entire directory. If you submit and are accepted to the ODP, it is only a matter of time before that link propagates itself onto the other websites that copy the ODP. Links from the ODP are among the most valuable on the Internet. Getting link from ODP can do more than anything to improve your pagerank. Remember! The ODP allows over 400 (estimated) other major websites on the Internet to copy their entire directory. If you submit and are accepted to the ODP, it is only a matter of time before that link propagates itself onto the other websites that copy the ODP. Links from the ODP are among the most valuable on the Internet. Getting link from ODP can do more than anything to improve your pagerank.

One of the original motivations for forming ODP was the frustration that many people experienced in getting their sites listed on Yahoo! Directory. However Yahoo! has since implemented a paid service ($299) for timely consideration of site submissions. That lead has been followed by many other directories. Some accept no free submission at all. By contrast the ODP has maintained its policy of free site submissions for all types of site — the only one of the major general directories to do so.

Make sure you submit your website to ODP! It is only a two-step process. Step-One: Select the best category for your site at dmoz.org and then click "suggest URL". Step Two: Follow the instructions on the submission form.

Chapter 8
THE LIST

Have Fun...

Now comes the fun part, submitting your website to over 800 search engines and web directories for yourself. Keep in mind that many of the search engines and web directories are free but some do ask for fees or reciprocal links. I encourage you to register your websites with as many as you can, starting with the "free" ones first. You may want to begin by submitting to only 20-30 search engines and web directories per day, because of all the search engines and web directories email notifications you will receive if you are accepted. You will need to open a corresponding email folder that will hold your confirmation and/or denial email letters from the search engines and/or web directories that you submit to.

To help you with this task of submitting your site, "the list" was produces in an excel spreadsheet format with columns that allow you to view the directory's free/fee status, Google's "PageRank", "check-off "column for you to check after you have submitted to a particular directory. The first seven listings are the general search engines and web directories that were recommended for websites owners looking to make a small investment in their link building campaign for a quicker indexing.

After these seven, the list in order of free search engines and directories, then PageRank and free/paid search engines and directories, then finally, PageRank.

Have Fun!

1-SEO WANTED

Search Engine/Directories	PR	Free/Fee
Dmoz.org	8	Free
Yahoo	9	$
Best of the web	7	$
Business.com	7	$
GoGuides	5	$
JoeAnt	6	$
Google	10	Free
2 Day Dir	0	Free
411.com	0	Free
Abc.com	0	Free
Apna.com	0	Free
Arakne Links	0	Free
Ask a Link	0	Free
ATTC	0	Free
Attracta	0	Free
Back Link Power	0	Free

THE LIST

Be Listed Now	0	Free
BizAds Business Locator	0	Free
Blue Daffodil	0	Free
Browsier.com	0	Free
Businesssearchonline. info	0	Free
deWWeb	0	Free
Directoryrecap.com	0	Free
Directoryy	0	Free
Findlink.com	0	Free
Free Best Websites Directory	0	Free
Free Stuff Sites	0	Free
freewebsitessubmission.net	0	Free
GraffitiLinks	0	Free
Greadadirectory.com	0	Free
Green Links	0	Free
HandiLinks	0	Free
HotBot	0	Free
HotLinks2	0	Free

Increase PR Directory	0	Free
InfoMarket	0	Free
Internet MeetingPlace	0	Free
IRD	0	Free
IsabelDeco	0	Free
j4r	0	Free
Jump Link	0	Free
Linkrain	0	Free
Majon	0	Free
Peekaboo.org	0	Free
Picked Sites	0	Free
Searchenginecolossus.com	0	Free
Stumbleupon.com	0	Free
thegres.net	0	Free
Toplinkdir.info	0	Free
Webtrafficgenie.com	0	Free
World index	0	Free
Xomreviews.com/pol arsearch	0	Free

THE LIST

Your WebScout	0	Free
1Ht.org	1	Free
A1 DirectorySearch.org	1	Free
A1 website	1	Free
About	1	Free
Americabest.com	1	Free
Art-ticlebox	1	Free
Avissoft network Web Dir	1	Free
Backlink Directory.co.uk	1	Free
Best Free Directory	1	Free
BigList.info – Free Web Dir	1	Free
BlossomDirectory.com	1	Free
Buy and Sell Online-	1	Free
Buy-it-Online.com	1	Free
Check It Out-	1	Free
Direct Find	1	Free
Dynamutt	1	Free
Etkal	1	Free

1-SEO WANTED

Ezinfo Directory	1	Free
Free Site Link	1	Free
Galactic Galaxy Star Search	1	Free
Greatdir.com	1	Free
Info.com	1	Free
Internet Yellow Pages Directory	1	Free
ispy.cc-Onlink Link Directory	1	Free
Just Another Directory	1	Free
Link Surplus	1	Free
Links Daily	1	Free
Lushina.com	1	Free
Lycos	1	Free
Making MoneyLibrary	1	Free
Mywebsearch	1	Free
Nicks Year	1	Free
Off Life	1	Free
Onpaco	1	Free
Premium Listing.org	1	Free

Pukt Directory	1	Free
Qlink Web Directory	1	Free
Quick	1	Free
Rank O Rama	1	Free
Regular Links	1	Free
So Red Hot	1	Free
Squidlinks.com	1	Free
Submitalink.net	1	Free
Summer Rains	1	Free
TopAdd	1	Free
URLMountain.com	1	Free
Wwindex	1	Free
Yoofindit	1	Free
Zomp	1	Free
100 Best Online	2	Free
2Space.net	2	Free
A List Directory	2	Free
Add URLs Free	2	Free
Adora.org	2	Free
Amplicast Directory	2	Free
Ask Bee Directory	2	Free
Assets Directory	2	Free

1-SEO WANTED

Ayogi	2	Free
Bee Directory	2	Free
Bueno Amigo	2	Free
Buy.net	2	Free
Can Links	2	Free
CDNet.org	2	Free
Crown	2	Free
Dear Links	2	Free
Detail Directory	2	Free
Directory Zeal	2	Free
Directory4Sites	2	Free
Enter The Web	2	Free
EVMINA Web Directory	2	Free
Explore List	2	Free
Fat64.net	2	Free
Find What Where.info	2	Free
Free directory	2	Free
Free Links Submit	2	Free
Free WebDirectory.co.uk	2	Free

THE LIST

general web directory	2	Free
General Media	2	Free
Global Directory	2	Free
Gray Directory	2	Free
HGTech Directory	2	Free
imom Links	2	Free
JJAE	2	Free
link Master	2	Free
linkDir.org	2	Free
Links SEO	2	Free
lydizin web Directory	2	Free
Mix Directory	2	Free
My Top Directory.info	2	Free
OneBestLink	2	Free
Oodir	2	Free
Open Link Directory	2	Free
OwnTruth.com/Directory	2	Free
PageRank Directory	2	Free
Pagerank.com	2	Free

PiggymooWebdirectory	2	Free
PDGuru.com	2	Free
Publimix.net	2	Free
Raiisa.com	2	Free
Red Lava Directory	2	Free
Registerlink.info	2	Free
Sams Directory	2	Free
SEO Link Pool	2	Free
Seo Range	2	Free
Seo Space.net	2	Free
Seo Web Dir	2	Free
Shapel	2	Free
Sighber Café	2	Free
Simple	2	Free
Sites Directory	2	Free
Sitesurf Directory	2	Free
Sri Gate	2	Free
Submit 2 Us	2	Free
Submit Directory	2	Free
Suggestyoururl.net	2	Free
Surf Yellow pages	2	Free

Syn Directory	2	Free
The Living Link	2	Free
The Robot	2	Free
VccLLc	2	Free
Vrok	2	Free
Wawa Directory	2	Free
WebFeeds.info	2	Free
wGs	2	Free
Wholesale Pimp	2	Free
Yess	2	Free
YVIR	2	Free
Zabalook	2	Free
Zeriouz.com	2	Free
474 Directory	3	Free
4ParentsToday	3	Free
6686.org	3	Free
A Simple Directory	3	Free
Ability Index	3	Free
All URLs.info	3	Free
Article Zones	3	Free
Auua11.com	3	Free

1-SEO WANTED

BackLink PartnerDirectory	3	Free
Bali	3	Free
Best Buy Deal	3	Free
Big Wig Biz	3	Free
BizCardz	3	Free
Business Resource	3	Free
Businesses On The Net	3	Free
Clixa	3	Free
CyberWiz	3	Free
Cyperspider	3	Free
Directory Global	3	Free
Directory Link	3	Free
Directory.am	3	Free
directorycritic.com	3	Free
Dmegs	3	Free
Dot Rig	3	Free
Enterwork	3	Free
Express-directory	3	Free
Fatinfo	3	Free

THE LIST

Finest 4	3	Free
Free Advertise	3	Free
Freedirectoriessubmit.com	3	Free
Fullerton Online	3	Free
Good Web Directory	3	Free
Hlnk	3	Free
HolidayDig	3	Free
Href Directory	3	Free
Index Web Romania	3	Free
Infignos	3	Free
Internet ExplorerSearch Site	3	Free
Invo.info	3	Free
Jorgensen Enterprises	3	Free
K-Links	3	Free
Link Dir 4u	3	Free
Link For Free	3	Free
Link Now	3	Free
Link777	3	Free
Linkcentre	3	Free

1-SEO WANTED

Linkdirectory.com	3	Free
LinkDirectory.com.ar	3	Free
Links Reference	3	Free
LiteDirectory.com	3	Free
Live 1.com	3	Free
MiriBlackDirectory	3	Free
Movie Digg	3	Free
M-S-N.org	3	Free
Netscape	3	Free
Network Room	3	Free
New Web Directory	3	Free
Niche-Listings.com	3	Free
Nintra	3	Free
One-Sublime-Directory	3	Free
openadp.com	3	Free
Pop-Net	3	Free
Profit Choice	3	Free
Purple Links	3	Free
Samaprzyjemnosc	3	Free
Sanory	3	Free

THE LIST

Save Look	3	Free
Search City	3	Free
Search Web World	3	Free
SEO Directory	3	Free
Seo Webtool	3	Free
Submit Link	3	Free
Submit Link.com.ar	3	Free
Submit Your Link	3	Free
The Great Directory.org	3	Free
The Vivid Edge	3	Free
Theseoking	3	Free
Thizzonline	3	Free
TopNetRanks	3	Free
TX6.org	3	Free
UltraOrganizer.com	3	Free
Viesearch	3	Free
Vinabet	3	Free
Vip Dig	3	Free
webhotlink.com	3	Free
Webolink	3	Free

1-SEO WANTED

Webworldindex	3	Free
Your Link Here	3	Free
Adaxas	4	Free
Amfibi	4	Free
Amray	4	Free
Ashe Web Directory	4	Free
Astanda DirectoryProject	4	Free
Banana Pages	4	Free
bIndexed	4	Free
Blogger Sites	4	Free
Cipinet	4	Free
Click My BrickDirectory	4	Free
CyberWebSearch	4	Free
Dal Net Ayuda	4	Free
Directory Storm	4	Free
Dramba	4	Free
eSiq Directory	4	Free
EXOspy.com	4	Free
GZZT	4	Free
HardSeek	4	Free

iJull	4	Free
Info Listings	4	Free
InterBis	4	Free
Jayde	4	Free
Letlink.co.uk	4	Free
Link Lair	4	Free
Little Web Directory	4	Free
Manic Media WebDirectory	4	Free
Media-Pros	4	Free
My Directory Live	4	Free
Netinsert	4	Free
Ohira Directory	4	Free
Onewaytextlink	4	Free
PakAdTrader	4	Free
Pedsters Planet	4	Free
Philly First on thefourth	4	Free
Rank BL	4	Free
Roask	4	Free

1-SEO WANTED

Sale	4	Free
Seekzap.com	4	Free
SEO Executive	4	Free
Seo Free Directory	4	Free
Sine Directory	4	Free
SonicRun	4	Free
Towersearch	4	Free
URL Shack	4	Free
uuDir	4	Free
WebNetClick	4	Free
West2002.org	4	Free
World Site Index	4	Free
Zunch Directory	4	Free
Buyer's Index	5	Free
CanDo Directory	5	Free
Comfind	5	Free
Coolshopping.com	5	Free
Dewa.com	5	Free
Email Announce	5	Free
eSearch	5	Free
Freelinksdirectory.net	5	Free

THE LIST

Info Tiger	5	Free
International Small Business Consortium	5	Free
ISPE Companies Index - scientific research	5	Free
JumpCity	5	Free
Ldmstudio	5	Free
Let's Link.uk.net	5	Free
Lexiconn	5	Free
One Mission	5	Free
Search Sight	5	Free
UBDaily	5	Free
Web Linker	5	Free
Wiki Web	5	Free
Worm	5	Free
YPO Free ListingSubmittal	5	Free
ArtPromote.com	6	Free
Askjeeves	6	Free
BizLink	6	Free
Bizweb	6	Free
Bloggapedia.BlogDirectory	6	Free
Enhance	6	Free
EntireWeb	6	Free

Fast Find	6	Free
Helpedia .org	6	Free
Linkmarket.net	6	Free
Megago	6	Free
Name	6	Free
PR.com	6	Free
Scrubtheweb	6	Free
Aaasmeeting	7	Free
Ask	7	Free
Big Book.com	7	Free
CalPoly Directory	7	Free
Cuil	7	Free
Four11	7	Free
Globo	7	Free
Hotfrog	7	Free
Iwon	7	Free
Tybit	7	Free
Web Directory	7	Free
WWAR	7	Free
WWWomen	7	Free
Bing	8	Free

Britannica	8	Free
Dogpile	8	Free
Excite	8	Free
Froogle	8	Free
Go.com	8	Free
InfoSeek	8	Free
Infospace	8	Free
MSN	8	Free
Webcrawler	8	Free
Yahooligans	8	Free
1 More Link	0	Free/Paid
2 Add Link	0	Free/Paid
24 Directory	0	Free/Paid
9dir	0	Free/Paid
Addurls.net	0	Free/Paid
Argentodo	0	Free/Paid

1-SEO WANTED

AWE.org	0	Free/Paid
Black Dhalia	0	Free/Paid
Black Directory	0	Free/Paid
Business Directory	0	Free/Paid
CrispyURL	0	Free/Paid
dARTdirectory	0	Free/Paid
Directory Choice	0	Free/Paid
Directory For You	0	Free/Paid
Guugl	0	Free/Paid
Its your Home Page	0	Free/Paid
Jumpinternet	0	Free/Paid
Just Another Link	0	Free/Paid
Linksation	0	Free/Paid
LookSmart	0	Free/Paid
Make Me Popular	0	Free/Paid
MaxBan	0	Free/Paid
MFG Info	0	Free/Paid
n6e.net	0	Free/Paid
Net Exchange	0	Free/Paid
NetLinksOne	0	Free/Paid

THE LIST

Nihongo YellowPages	0	Free/Paid
OMG.us directory	0	Free/Paid
Personal Home Page	0	Free/Paid
Picked Links	0	Free/Paid
Planetsearch	0	Free/Paid
Poke!.org	0	Free/Paid
Q3V.net	0	Free/Paid
RBSE-Spider	0	Free/Paid
Runes	0	Free/Paid
Searchenginessubmis sion.biz	0	Free/Paid
SiteFinder	0	Free/Paid
Smart Link	0	Free/Paid
Sunzine	0	Free/Paid
The Dive	0	Free/Paid
The Net Directory	0	Free/Paid
The New WorldWebdex	0	Free/Paid
Tradewave	0	Free/Paid
Unlock	0	Free/Paid
Web SearchUnlimited	0	Free/Paid
Web://411	0	Free/Paid
WebSearch (2)	0	Free/Paid

1-SEO WANTED

WebSearch(1)	0	Free/Paid
Websprinter	0	Free/Paid
WebVenture	0	Free/Paid
WhoWhere?	0	Free/Paid
World Market Links	0	Free/Paid
World Online	0	Free/Paid
1 Dir.co.in	1	Free/Paid
1414.info	1	Free/Paid
Ace Free Directory	1	Free/Paid
Ami Directory	1	Free/paid
B75.org	1	Free/Paid
Better Web Directory	1	Free/Paid
BlitzDirectory.com	1	Free/Paid
Dacoo.com	1	Free/Paid
Dir You	1	Free/Paid
Directory Bird	1	Free/Paid
Directory Lair	1	Free/Paid
Dmoz Killer Web Directory	1	Free/Paid
Domain-all	1	Free/Paid
Duwf	1	Free/Paid
FindSites.net	1	Free/Paid

THE LIST

Give Link.info	1	Free/Paid
Hichet	1	Free/Paid
Ilinkr	1	Free/Paid
Intra	1	Free/Paid
IwebInfo	1	Free/Paid
K1t.Org	1	Free/Paid
Link Plot	1	Free/Paid
Link Shade	1	Free/Paid
LinkFlame.com	1	Free/Paid
Linksert	1	Free/Paid
LinksM	1	Free/Paid
LinksWeb.net	1	Free/Paid
mdgr.com	1	Free/Paid
My Link Directories	1	Free/Paid
My Seo Directory	1	Free/Paid
Name Proz	1	Free/Paid
Notorious	1	Free/Paid
PR Web	1	Free/Paid
SEO Buzz	1	Free/Paid
SEO Free Links	1	Free/Paid
Site Directory 1	1	Free/Paid

The Best Damn LinksPage	1	Free/Paid
The Park	1	Free/Paid
The Vortex	1	Free/Paid
Udump.net	1	Free/Paid
URL Axis	1	Free/Paid
URL Backlinks	1	Free/Paid
UrlZilla.info	1	Free/Paid
Web Link Dir	1	Free/Paid
Web Links Home	1	Free/Paid
What's New (1)	1	Free/Paid
Whoopie	1	Free/Paid
Zimple	1	Free/Paid
01 webdirectory.com	2	Free/Paid
1 Bromley	2	Free/Paid
123 Hit Links.info	2	Free/Paid
2getfun	2	Free/Paid
99 Kat Directory	2	Free/Paid
a2adir	2	Free/Paid
Abc Directory.net	2	Free/Paid
Add Link Your	2	Free/Paid
Add New Link	2	Free/Paid

Add site Link	2	Free/Paid
Adicionar links sites add url seo	2	Free/Paid
AdvertMyCar.comDirectory	2	Free/Paid
Alist Directory	2	Free/Paid
AnyApex	2	Free/Paid
Avivafind	2	Free/Paid
AZ- Links	2	Free/Paid
Backlink	2	Free/Paid
BE41.com	2	Free/Paid
Best Links Directory	2	Free/Paid
bleaz.com	2	Free/Paid
Blogara.net	2	Free/Paid
BOOM! Directory	2	Free/Paid
BOOM! Directory	2	Free/Paid
Chanas	2	Free/Paid
Crawlr.org	2	Free/Paid
CTRL Directory	2	Free/Paid
Cvnord General Web Directory	2	Free/Paid
Dadaf	2	Free/Paid
Deep Linked	2	Free/Paid
Dexer.net	2	Free/Paid

1-SEO WANTED

Directory Master	2	Free/Paid
Directory Stop	2	Free/Paid
Domain LinkExchange	2	Free/Paid
Double Directory	2	Free/Paid
e—Links	2	Free/Paid
E-Web Dir	2	Free/Paid
Exalt Directory	2	Free/Paid
eXtreme-Directory	2	Free/Paid
Fast Directory	2	Free/paid
FBQE	2	Free/Paid
FBQO	2	Free/Paid
FF Directory	2	Free/Paid
Firstdir.info	2	Free/paid
Fishstates	2	Free/Paid
Frazzlet	2	Free/Paid
Free Directory Submit	2	Free/Paid
Free Submit URL	2	Free/Paid
Freeze	2	Free/Paid
General Directory 1	2	Free/Paid
Genius Link	2	Free/Paid
Gimme My Domains	2	Free/Paid

THE LIST

Go 2 Directory	2	Free/Paid
Greatdir.info	2	Free/Paid
HAQJ	2	Free/Paid
HRCE	2	Free/Paid
I Search Click	2	Free/Paid
India BusinessDirectory	2	Free/Paid
Internet Directory	2	Free/Paid
Join Weblink Society	2	Free/Paid
KEZF	2	Free/Paid
Kinds	2	Free/Paid
Kingdom of URL	2	Free/Paid
Land Lost	2	Free/Paid
Lazy Lucky	2	Free/Paid
Link Book .org	2	Free/Paid
Link Directory .TV	2	Free/Paid
Link Directory 1	2	Free/Paid
Link On Up	2	Free/Paid
Link Submit	2	Free/Paid
Link2.info	2	Free/Paid
Linkbeaver	2	Free/Paid
Linked Out	2	Free/Paid

Link-Orama	2	Free/Paid
Links Heaven WebLink Directory	2	Free/Paid
Links Here	2	Free/Paid
Linksdesktop	2	Free/Paid
List Your Website .org	2	Free/Paid
ManagerBiz	2	Free/Paid
Mega Links	2	Free/Paid
Mega Links Directory	2	Free/Paid
Modern	2	Free/Paid
My Free Directory	2	Free/Paid
My Free Directory	2	Free/Paid
My Search Place	2	Free/Paid
My Web Directory	2	Free/Paid
Net Improve	2	Free/Paid
Network ImproveDirectory	2	Free/Paid
New-Free Directory	2	Free/Paid
Nice Dir	2	Free/Paid
No Reciprocal	2	Free/Paid
Nuclear Land	2	Free/Paid
OIZB	2	Free/Paid
One Million Directory	2	Free/Paid

THE LIST

Online Marketing	2	Free/Paid
Online Url	2	Free/Paid
Painterbabu	2	Free/Paid
Planet server	2	Free/Paid
plus-uk.net	2	Free/Paid
Power	2	Free/Paid
PR3 Plus	2	Free/Paid
Productivus	2	Free/Paid
Romainia Index	2	Free/Paid
Rose Directory	2	Free/Paid
Ryo Website	2	Free/Paid
S B Links	2	Free/Paid
Seek Base	2	Free/Paid
Seo Directory Links	2	Free/Paid
SEO Directory World	2	Free/Paid
Seo Friendly WebLink Directory	2	Free/Paid
SirPac.org	2	Free/Paid
Site Bulk	2	Free/Paid
SiteAvenue	2	Free/Paid
Sitelinker.com	2	Free/Paid
Smart Dir	2	Free/Paid

Snofs Directory	2	Free/Paid
Spongy Web	2	Free/Paid
Stars Directory	2	Free/Paid
Submiturl.info	2	Free/Paid
Suggest URL	2	Free/Paid
Sysite Free Directory	2	Free/Paid
tcnmart.com	2	Free/Paid
The FreeDirectory.info	2	Free/Paid
The Free WebDirectory	2	Free/Paid
The Global Internet Index	2	Free/Paid
Tip Top Directory	2	Free/Paid
Top Directory 1	2	Free/Paid
Toplinesearch	2	Free/Paid
Total Link	2	Free/Paid
Tower Promote	2	Free/Paid
Triple W Directory	2	Free/Paid
Tywalls	2	Free/Paid
UB51	2	Free/Paid
uc33.com	2	Free/Paid
URL Directory 1	2	Free/Paid

URLD	2	Free/Paid
Web Directory 24.net	2	Free/Paid
Web Stuff	2	Free/Paid
Webs Link	2	Free/Paid
Website Maintenance Directory	2	Free/Paid
World	2	Free/Paid
World LinksDirectory	2	Free/Paid
Xigcl	2	Free/Paid
Your Net Directory	2	Free/Paid
Yourglobaltv.com	2	Free/Paid
Yuguofu.com WebDirectory	2	Free/Paid
ZBestLinks	2	Free/Paid
zTrenz Directory	2	Free/Paid
777media.comWhois	3	Free/Paid
A List Sites	3	Free/Paid
Add 2 Directories	3	Free/Paid
AddSiteFree.com	3	Free/Paid
agrieducation.org	3	Free/Paid
Ahewd	3	Free/Paid
All Sites Sorted	3	Free/Paid

Alternative healthdirectory.org	3	Free/paid
Best Site Directory	3	Free/Paid
Big-sites.net	3	Free/Paid
Blog Collector	3	Free/Paid
Counter Deal	3	Free/Paid
dbestdirectory	3	Free/Paid
Directory Vault	3	Free/Paid
Directory.Gtsee	3	Free/Paid
Domain Stations	3	Free/Paid
Domaining	3	Free/Paid
Enomal	3	Free/Paid
EnvironmentPageDirectory	3	Free/Paid
ErectADirectory	3	Free/Paid
ESG Site Directory	3	Free/Paid
Extreme Directory	3	Free/Paid
FAS Web	3	Free/Paid
Find 2K	3	Free/Paid
Find Some	3	Free/Paid
Forever Links	3	Free/Paid
Free 2 Find	3	Free/Paid
Free Online Directory	3	Free/Paid

THE LIST

Free SubmitLinks.info	3	Free/Paid
Free web linkdirectory	3	Free/Paid
FreeWebLink	3	Free/Paid
Funkylink	3	Free/Paid
Gain Web	3	Free/Paid
Golden LinksDirectory	3	Free/Paid
Good Links Directory	3	Free/Paid
Got Links	3	Free/Paid
Hitalyzer	3	Free/Paid
H-Log	3	Free/Paid
HRDW Directory	3	Free/Paid
Iixy	3	Free/Paid
Increase Directory	3	Free/Paid
India On The Net	3	Free/Paid
Inredllc	3	Free/Paid
iSearchLink	3	Free/Paid
Ismip 5	3	Free/Paid
Jfesc.com	3	Free/Paid
JHUCR	3	Free/Paid
JTOB	3	Free/Paid

Kaikus.com	3	Free/Paid
King of the Web	3	Free/Paid
Lace BusinessDirectory	3	Free/Paid
Link Centre	3	Free/Paid
Links Premium	3	Free/Paid
LinksHarbour.com	3	Free/Paid
List.com	3	Free/Paid
Live Urls .net	3	Free/Paid
Luton Engineering	3	Free/Paid
M. Directory	3	Free/Paid
Madhav Web	3	Free/Paid
MagDalyns	3	Free/Paid
Marketing Patch	3	Free/Paid
MOJOE	3	Free/Paid
MonsterDirectory.com.	3	Free/Paid
More Visits	3	Free/Paid
My Web Searches	3	Free/Paid
MyMoz.info	3	Free/Paid
NC Directory	3	Free/Paid
Neon Links	3	Free/Paid
Official Directory	3	Free/Paid

THE LIST

Online Web Directory	3	Free/Paid
Open Site Directory	3	Free/Paid
PB Lake	3	Free/Paid
Place 4 URLs	3	Free/Paid
Plenty of Links	3	Free/Paid
Premium Net	3	Free/Paid
Prlink Pop Directory	3	Free/Paid
Project Ultra	3	Free/Paid
Ricusa Seo	3	Free/Paid
Scoopfeed	3	Free/Paid
Seo Friendly	3	Free/Paid
Shadav .info	3	Free/Paid
Shocking Directory	3	Free/Paid
Skype Media	3	Free/Paid
SportDig	3	Free/Paid
Submit Site Now	3	Free/Paid
Submit Weblinks	3	Free/Paid
SubmitLink	3	Free/Paid
Suggestlink.com	3	Free/Paid
Tag Directory	3	Free/Paid
Tater links	3	Free/Paid
The Open Directory	3	Free/Paid

The-Free-Directory.co.uk	3	Free/Paid
Timgrendell FreeDirectory	3	Free/Paid
Top Sites	3	Free/Paid
TXTlinks	3	Free/Paid
U.K.D	3	Free/Paid
Vuwl	3	Free/Paid
Web Dir 1	3	Free/Paid
Web Directory 1 .info	3	Free/Paid
Web Duo	3	Free/Paid
WebLister	3	Free/Paid
Webmastercatalog.com	3	Free/Paid
Websitejoint	3	Free/Paid
WebVerve.com	3	Free/Paid
WL Directory	3	Free/Paid
Wondex	3	Free/Paid
World Web Directory	3	Free/Paid
Wuzle	3	Free/Paid
Yet Another Directory	3	Free/Paid
Yooley	3	Free/Paid
ZaBox	3	Free/Paid
Zopso	3	Free/Paid

THE LIST

A1 Web Directory.org	4	Free/Paid
AblazeDirectory	4	Free/Paid
Add URL Free	4	Free/Paid
Add Your site freesubmit	4	Free/Paid
Anaximander Directory	4	Free/Paid
All Link	4	Free/Paid
Boomlink	4	Free/Paid
CTAPDA	4	Free/Paid
Design-Agency.com	4	Free/Paid
Eigen	4	Free/Paid
Eliteweb	4	Free/Paid
Ethical Directory	4	Free/Paid
Exploratorius	4	Free/Paid
Find Top Links	4	Free/Paid
Free DIY SEO.co.uk	4	Free/Paid
Free Web Directory	4	Free/Paid
Link Add Url	4	Free/Paid
Links	4	Free/Paid
MallPark	4	Free/Paid
MarketSuite Mall -Bronze level is free	4	Free/Paid
PooZL	4	Free/Paid

1-SEO WANTED

Prospernet	4	Free/Paid
Red Directory	4	Free/Paid
Sites on Display	4	Free/Paid
Tag365 Directory	4	Free/Paid
Thales Directory	4	Free/Paid
The-web-directory.co.uk	4	Free/Paid
URLZ .net	4	Free/Paid
Vmoptions	4	Free/Paid
Web4URL	4	Free/Paid
Webaholics	4	Free/Paid
XHTMLValid	4	Free/Paid
Yourjoker.com	4	Free/Paid
ZA7.org	4	Free/Paid
ZeeZo.com	4	Free/Paid
Zero Directory	4	Free/Paid
A2Z Web Index	5	Free/Paid
BlogHints Blog Directory	5	Free/Paid
Expand	5	Free/Paid
Free Website Directory	5	Free/Paid
Gimpsy	5	Free/Paid
LinkMonster	6	Free/Paid

NetMall	5	Free/Paid
Overture	5	Free/Paid
Pegasus Directory	5	Free/Paid
Programming Resources	5	Free/Paid
Prolink Directory	5	Free/Paid
Pronett	5	Free/Paid
Web 100	5	Free/Paid
Where2Go	5	Free/Paid
Londovor	6	Free/Paid
MasterMOZ	6	Free/Paid
My Green Corner	6	Free/Paid
Nerd World	6	Free/Paid
OneKey	6	Free/Paid
SEO Court	6	Free/Paid
The Shoppings	6	Free/Paid
The Source	6	Free/Paid
What-U-Seek	6	Free/Paid
Access NewZealand.co.nz	7	Free/Paid
Alexa	7	Free/Paid
WhitePages	7	Free/Paid
Alltheweb	8	Free/Paid

1-SEO WANTED

AOL	8	Free/Paid
Digg	8	Free/Paid
Thomas Register	8	Free/Paid
AltaVista	9	Free/Paid
MegaByte Graphics Hot Links .org	0	Free/paid
MemoRandom	0	Free/paid
Baptism andChristening Directory	1	Free/paid
FreeDir.com	1	Free/paid
Internet AheadDirectory	1	Free/paid
4ON.org	2	Free/paid
A Free Directory.net	2	Free/paid
Another Directory	2	Free/paid
Fast Tracked	2	Free/paid
LinkMates	2	Free/paid
Link Hole	2	Free/paid
Worthful.info	2	Free/paid
Christian Directory	3	Free/paid
Free Bee Hut	3	Free/paid
Instant Web directory	3	Free/paid
Quality Submissions	3	Free/paid
Ablaze Directory.info	4	Free/Paid

THE LIST

Affiliate ProgramsDirectory	4	Free/paid
ATPPSA	4	Free/paid
Mergi	4	Free/Paid
Housenet	1	Free/Recip
Idorel	1	Free/Recip
Back Link Free	4	Free/Recip
000 Directory	2	Free/Recip/paid
Place Your Links	2	Free/Recip/Paid
Web Smart Ads	2	Free/Recip/Paid
Free Online Web Directory	3	Free/Recip/Paid/Deep
TuneCircle	3	Free/Recip/Paid/Deep
Directhits.org	0	Paid
e-vug.com	0	Paid
Submitedge.com	0	Paid
Tillads	2	Paid
Needmorehits	4	Paid
Groupweb	5	Paid

CONCLUSION

There is a sliver lining in all that had transpired over the six years since my friend Joya and I became contenders in the online world. We decided to make the best of a long journey into Internet marketing workshops, long conversations with customer services representatives in the website building process, getting the websites up and running, and pending learning Search Engine Optimization on our own. This book's evolution from conception one and is evidence by the introduction of two additional websites, 1seowanted.com PR0 and www.Colonlove.com PR3.

I hope that you will find much success and prosperity with your online business. Most import-antly, I hope you have gained an understanding of how the search engines and web directories work and how you can begin submitting to them yourself to increase your website's Internet presence and creating an ability to sell product/service and information. There are many opportunities that prove that anything is possible in the universe or shall I say, in "cyberspace." There

are unpredictability's as well. I would not have embarked on such a rewarding challenge had it not been for a pact I made with my friend to acquire a free gift. Well, that free business organizer has served as me well and revolved into a "do-it-yourself directory submission" instructional book that I hope will help many Internet entrepreneurs, small business owners and stay-at-home moms and dads discover how to create income using the Internet by making a presence for that creative and beautiful built website.

It will seem that all websites need backlinks to survive on the Internet Today. The more links your website have the better you will prosper, plus the more quality links you have the better your search engine rankings will become. Although there are several other factors that influence search engine rankings, link building through direct directories submissions is considered to be one of the most important of all. One of the simplest ways to build links to your site is by doing it for yourself by submitting your site to good quality web directories and search engines. Some of the search engines and web directories in chapter 8 will hold you captive for hours and some you may not wish to submit to, but by and large many are worth getting to know.

Often, Joya and I like to joke about how "Oprah Winfrey" will announce my name to her audience on the Oprah Winfrey Show or now, on "OWN". "Please, help me welcome, Mary Monteeeeeirooooooooo!" Don't stop dreaming. Grab your surfboard and prepare yourself to catch the big wave!

Appendix 1

Check for SEO-Friendly Factors:

At the time of writing this book, many of the search engines and web directories listed in chapter eight were "search engine friendly". The following instructions show how you can check to see if they do indeed still hold SEO – friendly status. Keep in mind that the Internet is always changing and it's constantly evolving. Years ago link building was just about getting as many links as you could. Now Google make websites who engage in the link building process be concerned with bigger stuff.

From the list of web directories compiled, you may want to make certain that they are search engine friendly before submitting your website. By this I mean that a directory will return links that are counted and valued by the search engines. Remember! The Internet environment is still rapidly changing. There would be no purpose in getting a directory link to your site if the links are not search engine friendly or 'SEO-Friendly'. If the links you get don't matter to the search engines, they won't matter to your website either! There are several things you should do to ensure that your links are SEO friendly:

Ensuring that there are no META no-follow or no-index tags on the link pages:

To do this, view the page source of one of the link pages in the directory. The page source can be viewed simply by right clicking your mouse while you are on the directories page. You will see an option that reads 'View Source' or 'View Page Source'. Click on the option to view the source code of the entire page. Within that page, look closely for the following code: <meta name="robots" con-tent="noindex,nofollow">

If you discover this code mentioned on the page, don't bother submit-ting your website to that particular directory, as the search engines would not count the links it gives out. Many directories like to build their own directories and do nothing for you're website in return, so you decide. When 'noindex' is written in the code, it basically tells the search engines not to index the page, while 'nofollow' tells the search engines not to follow or count the links on the page

Confirm that the links do not redirect to another page: Some directo-ries give out links that redirect to a page other than the home page. These links are not valuable as they are not direct links to the site. URL of the link pages should not contain too many parameters: An example of such a URL is:

http://www.webdirectory.com/link.php?u=23&as=2323434324& as=23423asfsfas&pw=32433.

Although this factor alone may not make a directory non-SEO friend-ly, it is believed that search engines either don't index or don't place too much value on those pages that have too many parameters in the URL. Only if a directory passes all these criteria, will it be considered a SEO-friendly directory.

Appendix 2
Glossary of Internet Terms

Acceptable Use Policy (AUP) – Rules that describe the kinds of activities that are allowed on a certain computer network.

Address – normally refers to one's e-mail, which can be a series of letters or numbers. When referring to a World Wide Web site, an address is the URL.

Anonymous FTP --A function that enables computer files to be shared among members of the Internet community without requiring the person who is making the request to identify him or herself to the owner of the remote computer system. This then allows the requesters to download a file from the remote computer.

Archie – A search program used to locate anonymous FTP files on the Internet. Once a file has been located using Archie, the person initiating the search may then use Anonymous FTP to retrieve it to his/her computer system.

ARPAnet—The network that was developed and funded by the Department of Defense. It preceded today's Internet.

Bandwidth—is a high-technical term used to describe the amount of data that can travel in a given time—usually one second— across a network or a connection to a network, such as a modem. When you send a message across the superhighway, you are using part of the Internet bandwidth, just as your car takes up space on the freeway/highway.

Baud or Bits Per Second (BPS)—a measure of how fast a modem can send and receive information; more is better. You will want a modem with a rating of at least 28,000 bps to access the Internet effectively, preferably, use a 56,000 (56k) modem. In most areas, high-speed access is available through the telephone company (DSL) or your local cable company.

Browser—refers to software that allows a user to navigate the World Wide Web. The two most popular Internet browsers are Netscape and Microsoft's Internet Explorer.

Broken Links-- A dead link (also called a broken link or dangling link) is a link on the World Wide Web that points to a web page or server that is permanently unavailable. The most common result of a dead link is a 404 error, which indicates that the web server responded, but the specific page could not be found.

Client—refers to a computer attached to any network, including the Internet. The term is also used to describe personal computer software that gives access to and enables the use of the Internet, either by modem connection or by connection to a local area network (LAN) and related hardware. A client can also refer to a program such as a web browser used to retrieve data, or a service, from a server on the Internet.

Conversion Rate—a marketing term that measures the percentage of orders from the total number of visits to a website over a period of time. Conversion rates on the web today average about 2 percent, meaning that a website will probably get two orders for every hundred people who visit the site.

Cyberspace—a popular term (first used by author William Gibson) for the space that seems to exist within computers and computer networks.

Domain Name—an Internet address. For example, 1seowanted.com. Currently there are six domain name extensions: .com is used for businesses, .edu for educational institutions, .gov for government agencies, .org for organizations, .mil for military, and net for networks. The domain name is an important part of all Internet addresses; e.g., name@domainname.com or www.domianname.com.

Download—the process of bringing data (text or graphics) from the Internet into personal computer.

Doorways—Doorway pages are Web pages designed and built specifically to draw search engine visitors to your website. They are standalone pages designed only to act as doorways to your site. Doorway pages are a very bad idea for several reasons, though many SEO firms use them routinely.

E-commerce—The ability to do business on the Internet by processing orders and taking payments from online buyers.

Electronic Data Interchange (EDI)—a standard format for exchanging business data that allows companies to place orders, bid on projects, and make payments over the Internet or over private networks.

Electronic commerce—also known as e-commerce; refers to sales or other business transactions over the Internet or over private networks.

E-mail—short for electronic mail; refers to messages sent from one person to one or more other persons over the Internet or a private network.

File Transfer Protocol (FTP)—a system for moving or copying files, such as programs, text or graphics, from a remote computer, called an FTP site, to another computer via the Internet.

Hit—A "hit" is a casual term indicating some measure of traffic to a web site .The problem with the term is that it can mean different things to different people under different circumstances. The most common use for the term "hit" means "visitors" or an actual person accessing a website. In almost every case, the term "visitor" is preferable to the term "hit." Most sophisticated web marketers don't use the term "hit" because of its imprecision.

Home page—the first, or main, page of a site on the World Wide Web, often leading to other pages. "Home page" and "storefront" are often used interchangeably.

Hyperlink—(or link) is a reference to a document that the reader can directly follow, or that is followed automatically. The reference points to a whole document or to a specific element within a document.

Hypertext—highlighted words on the World Wide Web pages that enable you to jump from one page to another without typing commands.

Hypertext Markup Language (HTML)—a special programming language used to make information compatible with the World Wide Web.

Hypertext Transfer Protocol (HTTP)—The set of rules for transferring files on the World Wide Web. HTTP allows people to navigate among documents or pages linked by hypertext and download pages from the World Wide Web. An http:// precedes every Website address.

Internet—a dynamic global network of computer networks that allows people to send e-mail messages, participate in discussions and access information without a central authority. The term is often used to describe the total body of interconnected computer networks.

Internet Service Provider (ISP)—is an Internet Service Provider. It is a company that maintains a constant connections to the Internet and sills Internet access to individuals and/or businesses. The term is also synonymous with Internet Access Provider, Access Provider and Access Service Provider.

Java—is a software language that allows people to build interactive Websites.

Jpeg—Common compressed format for picture files. Pronounced "jay-peg."

Link—a connection from one word, picture, or information object to another that can be selected with people click of a mouse. A Link most commonly appears as highlighted, underlined text, like this.

Local Area Network (LAN) – A collection of computers (usually not extending more than a few mile in diameter) linked together by phone lines or cables for the purpose of sharing information.

Lynx – A popular text-based Web browser.

Meta Tags-- A meta tag is a hidden tag that lives in the <HEAD> of an HTML document. It is used to supply additional information about the HTML document. The meta tag has three possible attributes content, http-equiv, and name. Meta tags always provide information in a name/value pair. The name and http-equiv, attributes provide the name information and the content provides the value information. Meta tags do not have a closing tag.

Modem—a device that allows a computer to connect to and communicate over telephone lines with another computer that is also connected to a modem. This is how most people connect to the Internet. The modem converts computer language that can be transmitted over ordinary telephone lines. It also decodes the language back to computer language when the message arrives.

National Science Foundation Network (NSFNET)—A network sponsored by the U.S. Government for the exchange of scientific research information.

Natural Search—Natural search listings (also called "relevancy listings") are the more traditional listings that appear below (and often also to the left) of the paid listings. Natural listings are totally free, but the key is that search engines decide which web sites get listed where in the natural listings based on several factors. i.e, PageRank, relevancy, keywords, keyword phrases, etc.

Net, The—A colloquial term that is often used to refer to the entirety of Cyberspace: the Internet, the commercial services, BBSs, etc.

Netscape—A browser for the World Wide Web that was designed with a Graphical User Interface (GUI) and hypertext links for easy navigation of the web. Microsoft's Internet Explorer browser is based upon many of its original designs.

Network—a group of computers linked together by a common communications protocol.

Newbie—a newcomer to the Internet, to an online game, or to an online discussion.

On line—Being connected (logged on) to a computer network service, such as America Online, CompuServe, or the Internet.

On line service—a service such as America online, CompuServe, Microsoft Network and Prodigy, which provides its members specific services. Originally, these online services provided e-mail, discussion groups and proprietary information. Many people confuse these services as being the Internet.

Page—A unit or organization of information on the World Wide Web. Information that is accessible via the Web (such as electronic storefronts) is organized and displayed as pages. A page may contain text, graphics, sound, and/or other elements.

Paid Search—Paid listings show up on the page because the website owner pays the search engines to put them there in the sponsored listings. The listings appear there based on a pay-per-click basis.

Protocol—a set of technical rules and standards for computer communication. Without protocols, computer networks could not exist, since the computers would not be able to communicate with each other in an intelligible manner.

Search Engines—World Wide Web sites that allow users to search for specific Web sites of interest by typing keywords or phrases. Popular search sites include Yahoo!, Google, MSN, Firefox, and many more. A search engine is a web site that helps people on the Internet find information or websites.

Server—a computer on the Internet that serves up files and information to Internet users (also called clients). Most people dial into a server that provides access to the Internet via a modem or over a network.

Spamdexing—(also known as **search spam**, **search engine spam** or **web spam**) is the deliberate manipulation of search engine indexes.

Storefront—term for an e-commerce enabled website on the Internet. Storefront is often synonymous with terms like website, home page, etc.

Rank—your rank in search results is where you appear in the search results. On a particular keyword phrase you might be ranked number 2. On another keyword phrase, you might be ranked number 30.

Real-Time—The Internet term for "live" as in "live broadcast".

Relevancy Search Engines—A relevancy search engine is what most people think of when they hear the word search engine. A relevancy search engine (like Goolge.com) maintains a huge farm of powerful servers that manage a gigantic database of the information contained on the web pages. When a person does a search on a relevancy search engine, that search engine compares the word searched, against the database of web pages. Then, based on the criteria set by the programmers who built the search engine, web sites that match up with the search words are displayed.

Uniform Resource Locator (URL)—The World Wide Web address of a resource on the Internet. It is important to type the address correctly. An extra space, a capital letter or a missing or additional period or slash will not work.

Usenet—A worldwide system dedicated to the dissemination of information made available on the Internet by the newsgroup service.

Visit—A visit, or a visitor, is an actual human being who comes to a website. The number of visits a web site receives per hour/day/month/year is the primary (but not the only) measure of traffic to a website.

Veronica—A search program similar to Archie, that searches the Gopher system menus to find information.

Web Browser—A program that enables World Wide Web locations (including electronic storefronts) to be viewed in a graphical, multimedia presentation style, often combining words graphics, animation, video, and sound.

Web Directory—One of several websites on the Web dedicated to creating a massive, human-edited, topical directory of websites on the Internet. The Open Directory Project is the largest and most important of the Live Directories.

Webmaster—The person responsible for creating and managing a Website on the World Wide Web.

Web page—A hypertext document that is part of the World Wide Web and that can incorporate graphics, sounds, and links to other web pages, FTP sites, gophers, and a variety of other Internet resources.

Web Site—A collection of Web document named by a unique URL or web address.

Wi-Fi—a high-speed wireless networking standard (at 11Mbps and increasing to 20Mbps). Wi-Fi is a leading RF technology backed by Apple and 3Com.

World Wide Web (The Web or WWW)—A series of thousands of documents found on the Internet, interconnected using a system of linked (hyper-text) words, allowing an Internet traveler to jump from one document to another in an unending process.

www.ingramcontent.com/pod-product-compliance
Lightning Source LLC
Chambersburg PA
CBHW071220050326
40689CB00011B/2383